T0184611

Beginning Unity Editor Scripting

Create and Publish Your Game Tools

Benny Kok

Apress®

Beginning Unity Editor Scripting: Create and Publish Your Game Tools

Benny Kok
Hong Kong, China

ISBN-13 (pbk): 978-1-4842-7166-7   ISBN-13 (electronic): 978-1-4842-7167-4
https://doi.org/10.1007/978-1-4842-7167-4

Copyright © 2021 by Benny Kok

Managing Director, Apress Media LLC: Welmoed Spahr
Acquisitions Editor: Spandana Chatterjee
Development Editor: Matthew Moodie
Coordinating Editor: Divya Modi

Cover designed by eStudioCalamar

Cover image designed by Pixabay

Distributed to the book trade worldwide by Springer Science+Business Media New York, 1 New York Plaza, Suite 4600, New York, NY 10004-1562, USA. Phone 1-800-SPRINGER, fax (201) 348-4505, e-mail orders-ny@springer-sbm.com, or visit www.springeronline.com. Apress Media, LLC is a California LLC and the sole member (owner) is Springer Science + Business Media Finance Inc (SSBM Finance Inc). SSBM Finance Inc is a **Delaware** corporation.

For information on translations, please e-mail booktranslations@springernature.com; for reprint, paperback, or audio rights, please e-mail bookpermissions@springernature.com.

Apress titles may be purchased in bulk for academic, corporate, or promotional use. eBook versions and licenses are also available for most titles. For more information, reference our Print and eBook Bulk Sales web page at www.apress.com/bulk-sales.

Any source code or other supplementary material referenced by the author in this book is available to readers on GitHub via the book's product page, located at www.apress.com/978-1-4842-7166-7. For more detailed information, please visit www.apress.com/source-code.

Printed on acid-free paper

*For those who try to make their editor look better
and forget to finish their game.*

Table of Contents

About the Author

Benny Kok is primarily a Unity asset publisher, indie game developer, and music producer. He is a creative individual who loves creating tools for Unity. He has published ProArray, Rhythm Game Starter, and BoneTool on the Unity Asset Store. He also dedicates his time to sharing open-source Unity tools on GitHub for the community.

Besides Unity, he has experience with app development, web development, 3D modeling, and music production. Previously, he created multiple open-source Android applications including OpenLauncher, PixerStudio, and River.

About the Technical Reviewers

Simon Jackson is a long-time software engineer and architect with many years of Unity game development experience. He's also an author of several Unity Game development titles. He loves to create Unity projects and he loves to lend a hand to help educate others, whether it's via a blog, vlog, user group, or major speaking event.

His primary focus at the moment is with the XRTK (Mixed Reality Toolkit) project. The goal of this project is to build a cross-platform Mixed Reality framework to enable both VR and AR developers to build efficient solutions in Unity and then distribute them to as many platforms as possible.

Sebastiano Cossu is a software engineer and game developer. He has worked on many AAA games on consoles, PCs, and mobile. He also contributed to the making of Total War: Rome Remastered. He is a lecturer at a prestigious Italian academy. He authored the Apress books *Game Development with GameMaker Studio 2* (2019) and *Beginning Game AI with Unity* (2021).

An immersive technology entrepreneur, **Abhiram A** is cofounder of Odyn Reality, an XR Tech startup. He is a Unity3D Ambassador for Unity India and doubles as an XR Coach for Pupilfirst Facebook School of Innovation. He was also part of Future Technologies Lab, Kochi as a Research Fellow in VR. He is a Udacity VR Nanodegree graduate and a Unity Certified Developer.

Acknowledgments

Writing a book is hard. It really is. But all of this wouldn't be even possible without Spandana Chatterjee first inviting me to write a book. Also, big thanks to Divya Modi, Matthew Moodie, and the technical reviewers and team at Apress! Finally, thanks to the Unity community, I would not be here writing this book without the motivation and supportive atmosphere from all of the peer developers.

Introduction

This book is about beginning editor scripting in Unity. I will go from very basic and simple methods of editor customization, such as using built-in attributes in your component script, to advanced methods like using UIToolkit and creating a custom EditorWindow in the later part of the book.

I will begin by introducing Unity and the Unity Package Manager in Chapter 1. I'll go over the current view of Unity's package and Asset Store ecosystem, and I will briefly talk about my experience with asset publishing.

Next, I will talk about using attributes and coding your custom editor with IMGUI and UIToolkit for your MonoBehaviour component in Chapters 2 through 4. In Chapter 5, you will create an Object Spawner Tool and look into the EditorTool API and using ScriptableObject.

Next, in Chapters 6 and 7, I will go through the details of my two assets, ProArray and Rhythm Game Starter, including the sales stats, how I prepared for the Asset Store submission, and the technical details of each asset.

Chapters 8 and 9 will be mostly about package workflow such as using Git with your Unity package, creating online documentation with GitBook or DocFX, and lastly distributing your package to platforms like GitHub, Open UPM, and the Asset Store.

So, what are you waiting for? It's time to create your game tool.

CHAPTER 1

Getting Started

If you are reading this book about custom editor scripting in Unity, I will assume you have already used Unity to create projects or games. Unity is one of the most popular 3D/2D cross-platform game engines in the game development market, and it is the foundation of many successful mobile, desktop, and even console game titles that you might have come across.

In recent years, Unity has expanded its reach into other industries, such as 3D animated films and AR/VR applications. Today Unity is not only a game engine; it's a flexible, real-time rendering technology. But what separates Unity from other game engines is the nature of Unity's extreme modularity and its flexibility in allowing developers to create custom tools that unlock new possibilities. This first chapter is an overview of Unity's Package Manager, editor scripting, and asset publishing. Let's get into it!

Unity's Modularity

Unity has been moving towards a fully modular structure since the introduction of the **Unity Package Manager (UPM),** shown in Figure 1-1, which is a system that handles package install, upgrade, versioning, and dependency resolution.

© Benny Kok 2021
B. Kok, *Beginning Unity Editor Scripting*, https://doi.org/10.1007/978-1-4842-7167-4_1

Figure 1-1. *Unity's Package Manager window allows you to search for different packages from Unity or other registries. You can also install assets from the Unity Assets Store*

With UPM, you can install Unity's latest packages with just one click of the Install button. You can also install packages via a Git URL that points to a repository hosted on GitHub or other Git providers; then the package will be installed automatically and managed by UPM.

Taking advantage of this level of modularity, Unity moved most of the core features into a package-based workflow. For instance, Unity's new rendering pipeline named **Scriptable Rendering Pipeline** (SRP) and two of the pipeline implementations are now installed via the UPM:

- **Universal Rendering Pipeline** (URP)

- **High Definition Rendering Pipeline** (HDRP)

Since each package can be updated individually without the need to bundle with the whole Unity binary, updates and bug fixes can be delivered faster on their own.

Unity is evolving with this modular approach. Unity created **DOTS** (Data-Oriented Technology Stack), which is a collection of packages revolving around the **ECS** (Entity Component System). DOTS is performance by default by utilizing multithreading technology under the hood. It also comes with some editor tools that make debugging and development with DOTS more accessible. For instance, the Entity Debugger views all of the systems and entity details for the Entities package (see Figure 1-2).

Figure 1-2. *The Entity Debugger in Unity DOTS's Entities package, showing all the systems and entity details in the world*

With the packages mentioned above, it's very common to see a custom GUI in the editor to help developers to view and edit the data for different scenarios. Editor scripting is becoming more and more useful than ever. By taking advantage of Unity's solid foundation, real-time rendering technology, and wide platform reach, you can build any custom tools on top of it, which could potentially speed up your existing workflow, solve specific problems, or introduce new features for development and thus unlock new possibilities.

Possibilities of Editor Scripting

Knowing how Unity Package Manager favors modular package development, it's time to look into some examples of the custom tools provided by Unity with editor scripting.

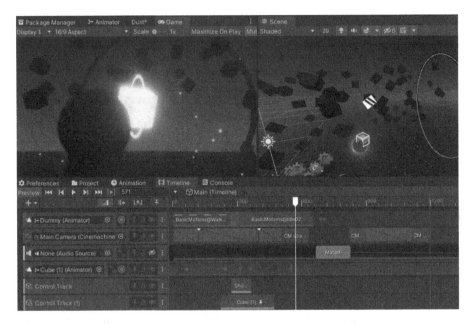

Figure 1-3. *Unity's Timeline Editor window, used in one of my personal projects*

First, let's talk about Unity's **Timeline**–a linear sequencer for animation and events (as seen in Figure 1-3). The concept is like a video editor's timeline, but with more game-centric functionalities. Timeline doesn't exist in earlier version of Unity. It is possible due to Unity's flexibility. It's written in C# with Unity's editor API, drawing the GUI with **IMGUI** (Immediate Mode GUI) and manipulating the data stored in the ScriptableObject for each clip's data. Now it's the go-to cinematic sequencer for game designers and essential tools used for 3D animated shots, such as Baymax Dreams by Simon J. Smith[1]. With Timeline, it's even possible to extend and create custom track behavior for various use cases via editor scripting and Timeline's API. It's a game changer for event sequencing in Unity, and once you learn about the basics of editor scripting, there are tons of possibilities.

---

[1]https://unity.com/madewith/baymax-dreams

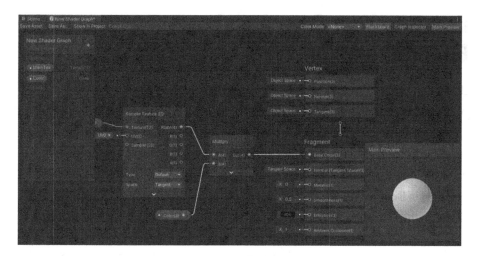

Figure 1-4. *Unity's Shader Graph editor window*

Secondly, Unity's **Shader Graph** (as seen in Figure 1-4) is an advanced shader editor tool by Unity. As mentioned, Unity introduced Shader Graph alongside the two major RPs; it's a node-based shader graph editor that will generate actual shader code base on your graph, allowing everyone to create shaders without coding in HLSL (High-Level Shading Language) and worrying about the compatibility for different rendering pipeline.

The Shader Graph is based on Unity's GraphView, which uses **UI Toolkit** (Unity's new UI solution for both editor and runtime) to leverage the flexibility of the GUI styling and complex layout under the hood. Developers can also extend on the GraphView API for different implementations and other use cases like custom dialog systems. The possibilities are endless.

Creating Your Own Asset or Editor Extension

Beside the official packages, there is the **Unity Asset Store**, a proven platform for publishing professional assets and editor extension, which saves developers tons of time with their projects. In the past few years, have been many success stories of asset developers making a living by creating custom tools and selling them on the Unity Assets Store. One of them is **Bolt**[2] **by Ludiq**, a visual scripting tool that was acquired by Unity in 2020 and became the official solution to visual scripting for the GameObject/MonoBehaviour workflow. Another one is **ProBuilder**[3] **by ProCore**, a modeling and level design package, which was acquired by Unity in 2018[4].

I am sure that you are not new to the Unity Asset Store. You might also come across other successful assets, such as **DoozyUI**[5]**,** a UI management system that streamlines UI management within Unity. I've been using it in a few of my projects and it really saves me tons of time when dealing with the UI state and animations. With Doozy's custom node editor and inspector, you're just a few clicks away from solving your problems.

So, you how do you get started with editor scripting and potentially publishing and selling your own assets in the store? Most of the time, the intention of the editor tool should be clear. Most likely you wanted to solve a specific problem in your own game project, so you went ahead and created a solution for it, and then you realized that other people might

---

[2]https://blogs.unity3d.com/2020/07/22/bolt-visual-scripting-is-now-included-in-all-unity-plans/

[3]https://unity3d.com/unity/features/worldbuilding/probuilder

[4]www.crunchbase.com/acquisition/unity-technologies-acquires-procore-tools--8ebcc38f

[5]https://assetstore.unity.com/packages/tools/gui/doozyui-complete-ui-management-system-138361

bump into similar problems and the solution you created could potentially save them time. That's where the value of the tool comes from, and when you see the value of the tool you created, you can consider packaging and publishing to the store. Who knows? It might become the next best-selling asset.

For me, one of my best-selling assets is **Rhythm Game Starter** (Figure 1-5), which is a rhythm game starter template. I developed it when I first attempted to create a rhythm mobile game back in late 2019. I had no clue that this asset would be a life-changing creation.

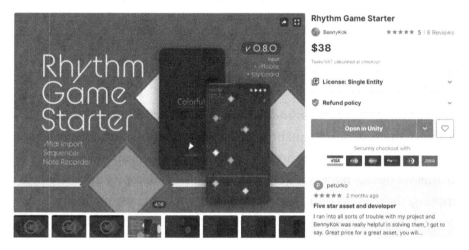

Figure 1-5. *Rhythm Game Starter's Asset Store page*

The first few months after I published this asset were amazing. Even though there were only 11 purchases in the first month (Figure 1-6), that was way more than I expected, compared to my previous asset's sales. For some reason, my assets appeared in the "Top New" assets section for some amount of time, and I am so blessed that the sales of **Rhythm Game Starter** were steady throughout 2020. I keep improving the experience with the asset and add a lot of custom tools to help people with their rhythm game projects.

January Sales		Gross $405.00			Net $283.50 (70%)			2020 January	⬍
Package	▲	Price	Qty	Refunds	Chargebacks	Gross	First	Last
ProArray - Array Prefab Placement	⊙	$25.00	3	0	0	$75.00	2020-01-05	2020-01-21
RhythmGameStarter	⊙	$30.00	11	0	0	$330.00	2020-01-11	2020-01-30

Figure 1-6. *Rhythm Game Starter's first month of sales details*

Even though it's not a huge number compared to other successful and best-selling assets out there, it's a good start to me. I will talk more about the details of each of my assets at a later stage of the book. Hopefully, it will give you insights into the potential of Unity editor scripting and how far it can take you.

What to Expect in the Book

In this book, my goal is to introduce you to editor scripting in Unity. I'll start from the very basics and how you can potentially use the knowledge learned here for your future projects and even publish your own assets, like me! While this book aims to cover most common topics around editor scripting, there exists more knowledge than you can really put inside a book, so I highly recommend you explore more on your own after reading this book.

I will start by introducing the fundamental way of customizing your component's inspector using the `Property` attribute and some common editor callbacks in `MonoBehaviour`. Next, I will talk about Unity's `GUILayout` & `EditorGUILayout` APIs, which is the traditional **IMGUI** (Immediate Mode GUI). You will create a custom inspector and custom editor window with IMGU.

Next, I will talk about Unity's **UI Toolkit**, a retained-mode GUI. UI Toolkit allows us to create an editor UI via code or with **UXML** (Unity eXtensible Markup Language) files and uses CCS-like stylesheets for stylings called **USS** (Unity Style Sheet). UI Toolkit doesn't have backward compatibility, meaning it's not available to older versions of Unity compared to IMGUI. However, it's becoming more stable and feature ready as an editor GUI. At this stage, UI Toolkit turns out to be pretty powerful and fun to play with, and with the **UI Builder**, a drag-and-drop UI builder for editing the UXML files, it is full of potential.

After introducing you to IMGUI and UI Toolkit, I will talk about some advanced editor topics, such as using `ScriptableObject` effectively. I will follow this with examples of extending the editor's scene view with `Handles` and registering custom `EditorTools` for interaction in the scene view. Also, I will talk about extending the preference window for custom settings with `SettingsProvider`.

Next, I will walk you through two case studies (ProArray and Rhythm Game Starter), explaining how the ideas for these assets came along and how I implemented specific editor features in detail.

Finally, I will talk about various ways to speed up your editor extension's development process, set up a documentation site for your package, and how you can distribute your editor extension submit to the Unity Assets Store or open source on GitHub as a UPM Git package.

Setup and Tips

Since this book is about the editor side of Unity, I assume you already know Unity to some extent and have Unity and a code IDE installed. Throughout the book I will be using **Unity 2020.2**. If you haven't, you can install it from the Unity Hub (Figure 1-7). For the Unity Hub, visit `https://unity3d.com/get-unity/download` to download.

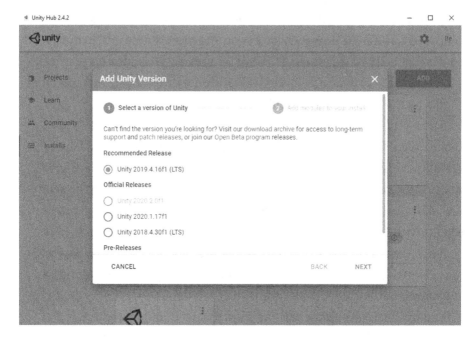

Figure 1-7. *Install Unity 2020.2 or higher from the Unity Hub*

I use **Visual Studio Code** (Figure 1-8) as my primary code editor on Windows. Feel free to open Unity and follow along. Additional Unity packages might need to be installed at later stages for specific examples.

Figure 1-8. *Download and install Visual Studio Code from* `https://code.visualstudio.com/`

To set up Visual Studio Code with Unity, you will also need to install the .NET core SDK and the C# extension in VS Code. Please refer to `https://code.visualstudio.com/docs/other/unity` for the latest detailed setup guide.

Among code IDEs, like Visual Studio or Rider by JetBrains, if you choose to use Visual Studio Code, there are few extensions that are useful for Unity. **Unity Code Snippets** (Figure 1-9) gives you many Unity-focused code snippets for autocompletion, even for creating custom editors.

Figure 1-9. *Unity Code Snippets*

Unity3D Meta Files Watcher (Figure 1-10) helps you to move the meta file of the script when you move the script inside VS code. It also handles script file rename and updates the corresponding the meta file, which

11

means this won't break the component references to your scripts inside of Unity, which is a lifesaver when refactoring your code in VS Code with Unity. Thanks to the authors!

Figure 1-10. *Unity3D Meta Files Watcher*

Finally, in a later part of the book, there will be topics on creating online documentation with docfx, which will require you to set up some extra command-line tools such as docfx and Node.js. You'll get more details in the specific chapters.

Summary

In this chapter, we walked through the overview of Unity's UPM with Unity's own packages, how editor scripting fits into place with asset publishing, and the overview of the scope of this book. In the following chapter, I will talk about the fundamentals of editor customization in Unity. Let's begin the journey!

CHAPTER 2

Customizing the Editor with Attributes and Callbacks

In this chapter, I will talk about the simplest way to customize your inspector experience in Unity. Starting from a simple C# `PlayerBehaviour` script as an example, I will walk you through the customization process by using the built-in C# `PropertyAttribute` in Unity. Next, I will talk about other useful attributes and some editor messages for `MonoBehaviour` that are useful for editor scripting.

Using the Property Attribute

In Unity, when you have a public or serializable field in your C# script that extends from `MonoBehaviour`, which is what you use to create custom components for the `GameObject`, the editor will reflect the corresponding UI in the inspector automatically for you (see Figure 2-1) to tweak the instance's values right in place. There are ways to customize it. The Unity editor comes with a brunch of C# attributes that allow you to modify how those fields are being drawn from the inspector. See Listing 2-1.

Listing 2-1. A Custom MonoBehaviour Class That Has a Float Field

```
public class PlayerBehaviour : MonoBehaviour {
    public float health;
}
```

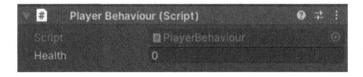

Figure 2-1. *PlayerBehaviour scripts in the inspector window*

In the sample code above, the health float field will be rendered as an editable float field in your inspector window. Next, I will walk you through some essential attributes to customize this script's editor.

The Range Attribute

The Range attribute will render the float/int field as a slider GUI (see Figure 2-2), requiring a min and max value range. It will clamp the input value in the editor. See Listing 2-2.

Listing 2-2. Using the Range Attribute

```
public class PlayerBehaviour : MonoBehaviour {

    [Range(0,100)]
    public float health;

}
```

Figure 2-2. The Range attribute displayed in the inspector

The Header Attribute

To group and better organize with the Header attribute, see Listing 2-3 and Figure 2-3.

Listing 2-3. Using the Header Attribute

```
public class PlayerBehaviour : MonoBehaviour
{
    [Header("Player Stats")]
    [Range(0, 100)]
    public float health;

    [Range(0, 50)]
    public float attackPt;
}
```

Figure 2-3. The Header attribute displayed in the inspector

15

The Multiline and TextArea Attributes

For a string field, you can have multiple lines and even a scrollable text area (Figure 2-4) with Multiline(lines) and TextArea (minLines, maxLines) attributes, as shown in Listing 2-4.

Listing 2-4. With Multiline and TextArea Attributes

```
[Header("Player Description")]
[Multiline(4)]
public string shortDescription;

[TextArea(4, 6)]
public string longDescription;
```

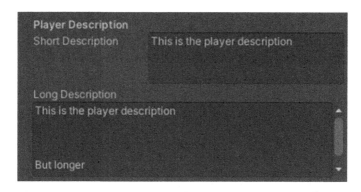

Figure 2-4. *The Multiline and TextArea attributes displayed in the inspector*

The Tooltip Attribute

Use the Tooltip attribute to add a description while you hover over that field in the inspector, as shown in Listing 2-5 and Figure 2-5.

Listing 2-5. Using the Tooltip Attribute

```
[Tooltip("Should we use the long description...")]
public bool useLongDescription;
```

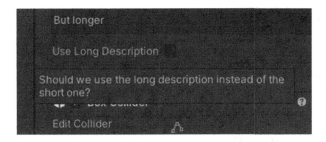

Figure 2-5. *Tooltip will show upon mouse hover*

The HideInInspector Attribute

To hide a specific public or `SerializeField` private from the inspector, use the `HideInInspector` attribute. It will not be shown in the inspector while the value is still being serialized. See Listing 2-6.

Listing 2-6. Using the HideInInspector Attribute

```
[HideInInspector]
public bool hiddenBool;
```

The SerializeField Attribute

When you have a private field in your component class but you still want Unity to show that specific field in the inspector, use the `SerializeField` attribute. This way you can enforce encapsulation of the class's data while still allowing the values to be tweaked in the editor. See Listing 2-7.

Listing 2-7. Using the HideInInspectorAttribute

```
[SerializeField]
private bool privateSerialiedField;
```

The Space Attribute

Use the Space Attribute to add a slight separation between the previous and current property. See Listing 2-8 and Figure 2-6.

Listing 2-8. Using the Space Attribute

```
[Space, SerializeField]
private bool privateSerializedField;
```

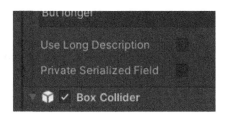

Figure 2-6. *Using the Space attribute*

Other Useful Attributes

Beside the C# attributes used to modify how the script member is drawn in the inspector, there are other useful attributes that let you hook into other parts of the Inspector so you can add in extra functionality.

ContextMenu

It's super useful to have an extra menu item for your component to execute code right from the inspector. The ContextMenu attribute will add menu items to the context menu of the component (see Listing 2-9 and Figure 2-7). Useful scenarios could be a custom method to randomly fill in some values for the player or to auto-assign specific values to your component.

Listing 2-9. Using ContextMenu Attribute on a Method

```
[ContextMenu("Randomize Player Stats")]
public void RandomizePlayerStats()
{
    health = Random.Range(0, 101);
    attackPt = Random.Range(0, 51);
}
```

Figure 2-7. *The context menu appears when you press on the three-dot button on the component header*

The HelpURL Attribute

With most built-in components from Unity, when you click on the question mark icon button in the top right-hand corner (Figure 2-8) you are directed to Unity's documentation site. With the HelpURL attribute, you can customize the link to your own documentation site; see Listing 2-10.

Listing 2-10. Using the HelpURL Attribute on the MonoBehaviour
Subclass

```
[HelpURL("https://docs.unity3d.com/")]
public class PlayerBehaviour : MonoBehaviour { }
```

Figure 2-8. *The question mark button will open the link in your
browser*

AddComponentMenu

With the AddComponentMenu attribute added to your MonoBehaviour, you
can specify a path for the component in the Add Component menu from
the inspector and it will appear under the corresponding path in the menu
(Figure 2-9). This will also modify the component name displayed in the
inspector (Figure 2-10). Use the code in Listing 2-11.

Listing 2-11. Using the AddComponentMenu Attribute on the
MonoBehaviour Subclass

```
[AddComponentMenu("Game/Player Behaviour")]
public class PlayerBehaviour : MonoBehaviour { }
```

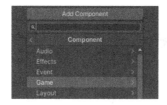

Figure 2-9. *The component can be found under the path you defined*

Figure 2-10. *The component name will also be changed in the inspector*

You can hide your component from the menu by passing in an empty string in the attribute. See Listing 2-12 and Figure 2-11.

Listing 2-12. Using the AddComponentMenu Attribute to Hide the Component from the Menu

```
[AddComponentMenu("")]
```

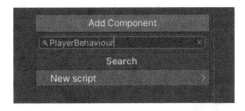

Figure 2-11. *The component is hidden from the Add Component menu*

ExecuteAlways

You may want to execute a script in edit mode for some edit-time behavior. You can do so by marking it with ExecuteAlways. Then, for example, your script's Update method will be called even if the game is not playing. See Listing 2-13.

21

Listing 2-13. Using the ExecuteAlways Attribute on the
MonoBehaviour Subclass

```
[ExecuteAlways]
public class PlayerBehaviour : MonoBehaviour { }
```

RequireComponent

Use `RequireComponentAttribute` if your component depends on another
component, such as `[RequireComponent(typeof(Rigidbody))]`. For
example your `PlayerBehaviour` might depend on a `RigidBody` component.
With this attribute, when adding the component in the inspector, if the
existing component doesn't exist, Unity will add it for you. It will also
prompt you (Figure 2-12) if you are removing the required component
(`Rigidbody` in this case) and it can only be removed when there aren't any
components requiring it, so you must remove the `PlayerBehaviour` first.

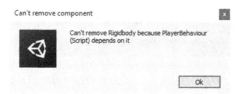

Figure 2-12. *When removing a required component, a dialog will
prompt outv*

MonoBehaviour Editor Messages

Apart from the attributes that let you easily customize the inspector's look
and behavior, there are some editor-specific messages for `MonoBehaviour`
that let you do some extra stuff in the editor.

OnValidate

OnValidate is called from the editor when any of the fields are being tweaked in the inspector. It is very useful to add custom validation logic to the inspector. For instance, Listing 2-14 shows how to display a log when the attackPt is larger than the health. It's probably not the best way to display a warning, but we will talk about this more in the following chapters when creating a custom editor.

Listing 2-14. Implementing an OnValidate Callback

```
private void OnValidate()
{
    //Example validation use case
    if (attackPt > health)
    {
        Debug.Log("Hp can't be larger than attack point.");
    }
}
```

OnDrawGizmos

In Unity, you can draw extra gizmos for your component. See Listing 2-15 and Figure 2-13. The gizmos are selectable in the editor and useful to help users quickly visualize the target GameObject.

Listing 2-15. Implementing an OnDrawGizmos Callback

```
private void OnDrawGizmos()
{
    //Always draw a wired sphere
    Gizmos.DrawWireSphere(transform.position, 5);
}
```

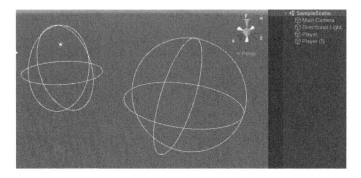

Figure 2-13. *Example of drawing a wire sphere gizmo in the scene view*

OnDrawGizmosSelected

Like OnDrawGizmos, but the OnDrawGizmosSelected method will only be called when the current GameObject is being selected in the editor. See Listing 2-16 and Figure 2-14.

Listing 2-16. Implementing an OnDrawGizmosSelected Callback

```
private void OnDrawGizmosSelected()
{
    //Draw a sphere only when selected
    Gizmos.DrawSphere(transform.position, 2);
}
```

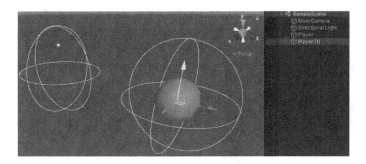

Figure 2-14. *Example of drawing a solid sphere gizmo when the object is selected*

Note   For more details about the `Gizmos` class, you can reference Unity's documentation[1] about it. For instance, beside `DrawSphere`, you can use `DrawLine` and `DrawIcon`.

Reset

Each component has a reset function in the menu (Figure 2-15), which basically resets the component values to the defaults. However, you can have custom reset logic by creating a `Reset` method in your component, and it will get called when you invoke the reset item in the menu. See Listing 2-17.

Listing 2-17. Implementing a Reset Callback

```
private void Reset()
{
    health = 10;
    attackPt = 5;
    shortDescription = "Default Description";
}
```

---

[1]https://docs.unity3d.com/ScriptReference/Gizmos.html

Figure 2-15. *The Reset menu item in the context menu of the component in the inspector*

Note   Reset will be also called when the component is first added to the GameObject in the editor.

Summary

In this chapter, you learned about using Unity's built-in C# PropertyAttribute to easily modify how the component's editor is displayed in the inspector. For instance, a RangeAttribute will have the float and int fields rendered as sliders in the editor, and a HeaderAttribute will render a header title with some spacing above that property. Next, you learned that there are some editor-specific messages for `MonoBehaviour`, such as the `OnValidate` method, which is useful for checking for the data inputted in the inspector, and the `Reset` method for resetting or initializing some fields in the components.

In the next chapter, I will talk about how you can create your own custom editors, attributes, and editor windows.

CHAPTER 3

Custom Editor with IMGUI

Now that you have learned some helpful editor attributes and editor-specific messages in MonoBehaviour, it's time to dive into coding a custom GUI yourself.

With Unity Editor, the majority of the GUI can be created with the EditorGUILayout and GUILayout classes under the hood. They are immediate mode GUI classes with an automatic layout calculation built on top of the EditorGUI and GUI classes, and they provide a straightforward way of GUI drawing. By design, each line of IMGUI code should be called every time to output the graphic onto the screen. It's a fairly low-level way of doing the GUI while giving you the maximum level of freedom and control over how you draw everything.

While most of the basic customization can be done using property attributes such as HeaderAttribute and RangeAttribute, for a more customized Editor experience, it's easier to code it the way you want it. Let's get started!

© Benny Kok 2021
B. Kok, *Beginning Unity Editor Scripting*, https://doi.org/10.1007/978-1-4842-7167-4_3

Differences Between Editor Scripts and Normal C# Scripts

Before you start, you need to know the differences between editor scripts, which involve the usage of the UnityEditor namespace, and normal runtime scripts. You usually create runtime C# scripts in Unity and extend the MonoBehaviour class, which uses the UnityEngine namespace. This way Unity knows that the script is a component and will let you attach the script to a GameObject. Without a specification, all your C# scripts in the project will be taken into account for the compilation of the final build. Therefore, you don't want your editor scripts to be included into the build. With editor scripts, you use the UnityEditor namespace for specific editor classes, but all of the code under the UnityEditor namespace will not be included in your final build, so you must make sure that your editor code is also being excluded from the build. There are multiple ways to solve this problem. Let's talk about them!

Editor Folder

First, for any folder that is named Editor (Figure 3-1), all the C# files inside it will be treated as editor scripts (scripts that only run in the editor) and will be excluded from the final build, which is exactly what you want. It's standard practice to have the editor code separated into an Editor folder.

Figure 3-1. *Separating editor scripts into an Editor folder*

Custom Editor Script Example

A typical custom editor script for extending the editor of a component is put into the Editor folder and you usually extend from the UnityEditor. Editor class. Then, by marking it with a CustomEditor attribute to target a MonoBehaviour type, you can override the Inspector GUI of that component. See Listing 3-1.

Listing 3-1. An Editor Script for a Custom Editor

```
using UnityEditor;

[CustomEditor(typeof(PlayerBehaviour))]
public class PlayerBehaviourEditor : Editor
{
    public override void OnInspectorGUI()
    {
        // You editor GUI code here
    }
}
```

#if Preprocessor

Next, in C# there is a thing called a preprocessor directive, which you can utilize to allow some code to be ignored or included in a compilation if a specific symbol is defined:

```
#if UNITY_EDITOR
// Your editor code goes here
#endif
```

In Unity, there are Unity-specific symbols defined for different editor platforms and target platform compilations:

- UNITY_EDITOR (will be defined if the code is compiling for an editor)

- UNITY_IOS (will be defined if the code is compiling for an iOS player)

- UNITY_ANDROID (will be defined if the code is compiling for an Android player)

- ...

For the full list of Unity's platform #define directives, please refer to Unity's online documentation[1].

Therefore, with the UNITY_EDITOR symbol, you can use the #if preprocessor to wrap around your custom editor code right in the same runtime script file, which is way more convenient than having a separate editor script file in the Editor folder.

Listing 3-2 shows the custom editor code in the same runtime script file. First, you use the UnityEditor namespace by wrapping a #if UNITY_EDITOR around the using namespace code. Note that each #if should end with a #endif. Next, you can include the editor code in the same file, by also wrapping the editor-specific code with the #if UNITY_EDITOR and #endif block.

Listing 3-2. EnemyBehaviour with EnemyBehaviourEditor in the Same File

```
using UnityEngine;
#if UNITY_EDITOR
using UnityEditor;
#endif
```

---

[1]https://docs.unity3d.com/Manual/PlatformDependentCompilation.html

```
public class EnemyBehaviour : MonoBehaviour
{
    public float health;

    public float attackPt;
}

#if UNITY_EDITOR
[CustomEditor(typeof(EnemyBehaviour))]
public class EnemyBehaviourEditor : Editor
{
    public override void OnInspectorGUI()
    {
        // You editor GUI code here
    }
}
#endif
```

Assembly Definitions

Next, let's talk about using Assembly Definition (asmdef), which is already a common practice for Unity's official packages. Assembly is a .NET concept, which is a compiled output of your code, usually a DLL file. Sound familiar? Since Unity uses C# from .NET, under the hood all your C# code is compiled into DLL files and cached in the library folder (Figure 3-2), so your code can run in the editor. Using asmdef in Unity allows you to separate your package code into individual Assembly output, which enforces code separation between different packages and prevents you from accessing code in other Assemblies without explicitly defining it in the .asmdef. I will talk about how to create an Assembly Definition in the following section.

Name	Date modified	Type	Size
Assembly-CSharp-Editor.dll	12/22/2020 5:24 PM	Application exten...	7 KB
Assembly-CSharp-Editor.pdb	12/22/2020 5:24 PM	PDB File	2 KB
BuiltinAssemblies.stamp	12/22/2020 5:24 PM	STAMP File	1 KB
com.bennykok.hierarchy-header.dll	12/22/2020 5:24 PM	Application exten...	4 KB
com.bennykok.hierarchy-header.editor.dll	12/22/2020 5:24 PM	Application exten...	11 KB
com.bennykok.hierarchy-header.editor.p...	12/22/2020 5:24 PM	PDB File	3 KB
com.bennykok.hierarchy-header.pdb	12/22/2020 5:24 PM	PDB File	1 KB
CutomTools.Runtime.dll	12/22/2020 5:24 PM	Application exten...	10 KB
CutomTools.Runtime.pdb	12/22/2020 5:24 PM	PDB File	2 KB
Unity.CollabProxy.Editor.dll	12/22/2020 5:24 PM	Application exten...	152 KB
Unity.CollabProxy.Editor.pdb	12/22/2020 5:24 PM	PDB File	42 KB
Unity.Rider.Editor.dll	12/22/2020 5:24 PM	Application exten...	71 KB
Unity.Rider.Editor.pdb	12/22/2020 5:24 PM	PDB File	21 KB
Unity.TextMeshPro.dll	12/22/2020 5:24 PM	Application exten...	376 KB
Unity.TextMeshPro.Editor.dll	12/22/2020 5:24 PM	Application exten...	209 KB
Unity.TextMeshPro.Editor.pdb	12/22/2020 5:24 PM	PDB File	60 KB
Unity.TextMeshPro.pdb	12/22/2020 5:24 PM	PDB File	154 KB
Unity.Timeline.dll	12/22/2020 5:24 PM	Application exten...	125 KB

Figure 3-2. *The compiled DLL files in your project's cache folder >*
Library > ScriptAssemblies

By default, all your runtime scripts go into `Assembly-CSharp.dll` while
your editor scripts under the `Editor` folder go into `Assembly-CSharp-`
`Editor.dll` (Figure 3-3).

Figure 3-3. *The default Assemblies for your scripts*

The goal is to have a cleaner structure among multiple packages. So if
all of the Unity package's compiled code goes into the default Assembly,
it will be coupled together and hard to manage, and if you change one of
your scripts, the entire Assembly will need to be recompiled. Separating
your scripts into a corresponding Assembly will speed up the compilation

speed since only the Assembly your script belongs to needs to be recompiled. In a large project, it's a must!

Associating your scripts with a separate Assembly is very easy. Right-click your scripts' folder and then click Create. Look for Assembly Definition (Figure 3-4).

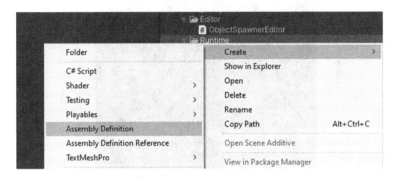

Figure 3-4. *Creating an Assembly Definition*

After the Assembly Definition file is created, you usually have one for the Runtime scripts folder and another one for your Editor scripts folder, as in Figure 3-5. The scripts under that folder will be associated automatically.

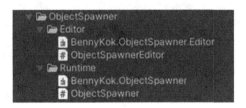

Figure 3-5. *Folder structure for the Assembly Definition*

Tip   To learn more about the folder structure convention used by the Unity official package, go to https://docs.unity3d.com/Manual/cus-layout.html.

Now, the important part: In the inspector for the editor asmdef, you must only select Editor in the platform section (Figure 3-6).

Figure 3-6. *Platforms section of the asmdef inspector*

Reference your runtime asmdef under the Assembly Definition References (Figure 3-7), and make sure to hit the Apply button after the changes.

Figure 3-7. *Assembly Definition Reference section of the asmdef inspector*

With Assembly Definition, you must manage other Assembly references manually. For instance, if your scripts must use the Unity. TextMeshPro package, you must reference its Assembly Definition to yours. This makes sure the dependencies between each package are crystal clear. Lastly, by default all other Assemblies in the project are auto-referenced to Assembly-CSharp, which if you mean to have the scripts inside your custom Assembly to reference those in the default Assembly, there will be a circular dependency, which is not possible by design. You might need to reconsider your code's design pattern to avoid this problem.

Note   To learn more about asmdef, Unity's documentation is pretty detailed. You can find it at `https://docs.unity3d.com/Manual/ScriptCompilationAssemblyDefinitionFiles.html`.

Custom Editor

Now that you know that there are different ways to handle editor scripts, you will use the `#if` preprocessor for this example to keep it simple and self-contained in a single script for now. Based on the `EnemyBehaviour` example in Listing 3-2, let's try adding a custom GUI button that is going to select all of the existing enemies in the scene for the `EnemyBehaviour` component so you can edit all of the enemies at the same time.

In the following `OnInspectorGUI` method (Listing 3-3), you do a base call to the parent editor class's `OnInspectorGUI` to draw the default UI. Next, you draw a button with `GUILayout.Button` and pass in the button's name. It will return a `boolean` indicating whether the button has been pressed. Then you can look for the `EnemyBehaviour` component by the `FindObjectsOfType` method and pass the target `GameObjects` to the `Selection` class, which allows you to change the active selection of the editor. The custom editor will now look like Figure 3-8.

Listing 3-3. Drawing a Button in the Inspector That Will Select the GameObject That Has the EnemyBehaviour Component

```
public override void OnInspectorGUI()
{
    base.OnInspectorGUI();

    if (GUILayout.Button("Select all enemies"))
    {
        var allEnemyBehaviour = GameObject.FindObjectsOfType
        <EnemyBehaviour>();
        var allEnemyGameObjects = allEnemyBehaviour
            .Select(enemy => enemy.gameObject)
            .ToArray();
        Selection.objects = allEnemyGameObjects;
    }
}
```

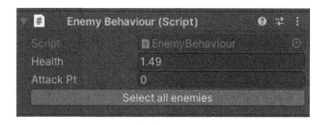

Figure 3-8. *Custom editor with a button*

CanEditMultipleObjects

However, when you click the "Select all enemies" button, you will see that "Multi-object editing not supported" (Figure 3-9). Oops! It seems like something is missing. Let's get back to the editor class and add a CanEditMultipleObjects attribute (Listing 3-4) to indicate that your custom editor supports editing multiple objects at the same time.

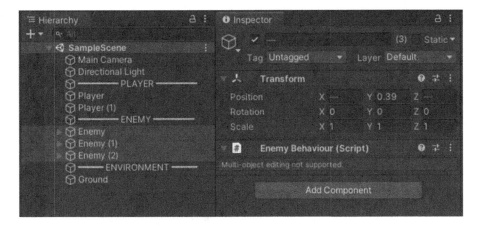

Figure 3-9. *"Multi-object editing not supported" message when more than one enemy is selected*

Listing 3-4. Adding the CanEditMultipleObjects Attribute to the Custom Editor Class

```
[CustomEditor(typeof(EnemyBehaviour)), CanEditMultipleObjects]
```

Note   If your custom editor has code that breaks multi-object editing, don't use the `CanEditMultipleObjects` attribute.

Click the button again. All of the enemies in the scene will be selected and the custom editor should be displayed correctly. Now you can easily edit all of the enemies at the same time.

IMGUI Debugger

Before we move on to more complex layout drawings, let's take a look at the IMGUI Debugger, which is helpful for inspecting the layout and drawing sequence of the IMGUI calls in the editor along the way. Under Window > Analysis > IMGUI Debugger, you will see the debugger for IMGUI (Figure 3-10).

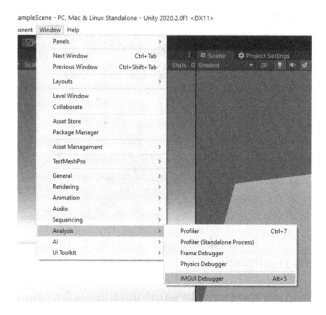

Figure 3-10. *The menu location of the IMGUI Debugger*

Once you open it, you can choose the target window to inspect in the drop-down menu (Figure 3-11).

Figure 3-11. *Selecting the Inspector view of the IMGUI Debugger*

Alternatively, you can hold the Pick Style button over the top right corner (Figure 3-12) and then slide to the GUI part you want to inspect in the editor.

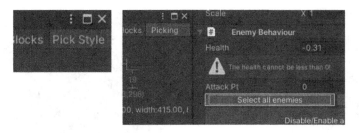

Figure 3-12. *Picking the GUI directly*

When the GUI is highlighted, you can let go and it will be selected. Now you can see the specific IMGUI call sequence, the line that the code was called in scripts, the rect size, GUIContent (the class holding GUI text, tooltip, and icon information), etc. in the IMGUI Debugger (Figure 3-13).

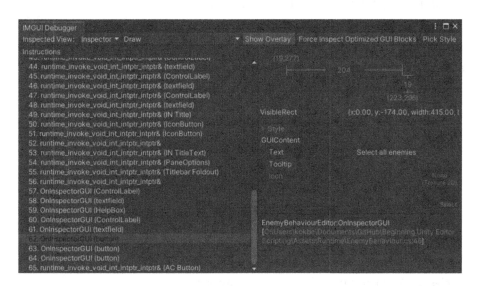

Figure 3-13. *IMGUI Debugger window*

Moreover, you can view the specific instruction chain of the inspected window (Figure 3-14), such as the property calls and so on.

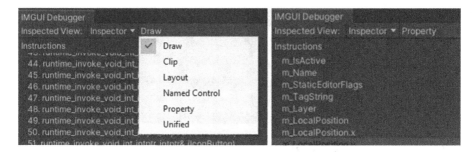

Figure 3-14. *Filtering different instruction chains*

Editor GUI Layout

Based on the previous EnemyBehaviour custom editor and your button code in Listing 3-3, let's look into more layout options. Let's add one more button that clears the object selection (Figure 3-15). To place it next to the one you just added, you need wrap the code between a BeginHorizontal call and a EndHorizontal call from the EditorGUILayout class. Let's wrap the code around the GUILayout.Button call (Listing 3-5).

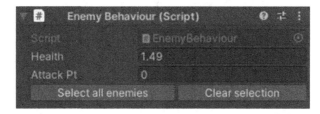

Figure 3-15. *Horizontal layout with two buttons*

Listing 3-5. Drawing a Horizontal Layout

```
EditorGUILayout.BeginHorizontal();

if (GUILayout.Button("Select all enemies")) { ... }

if (GUILayout.Button("Clear selection"))
```

```
{
    Selection.objects = new Object[] { (target as
    EnemyBehaviour).gameObject };
}
```

EditorGUILayout.EndHorizontal();

However, it gets cumbersome if your editor layout gets more complex and sometimes you may forget to close the layout with the End method. Luckily, Unity has various disposable scopes (Figure 3-16) that let you do the layout code in a much cleaner syntax with C#'s using statement. For example, let's use the HorizontalScope in Listing 3-6, and correspondingly VerticalScope can be used for wrapping a vertical layout.

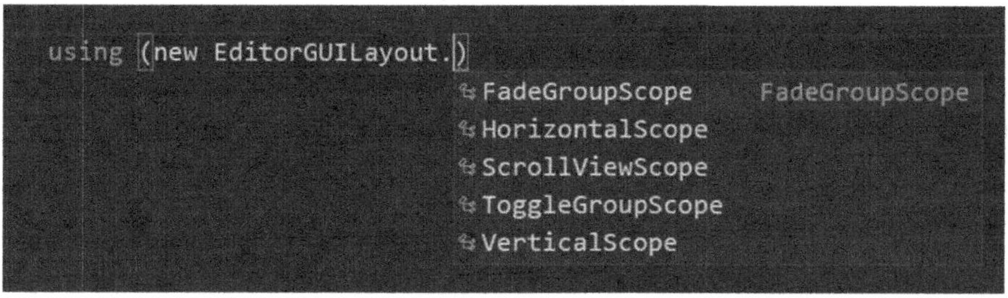

Figure 3-16. *Different built-in layout scopes*

Listing 3-6. Using Statement with HorizontalScope

```
using (new EditorGUILayout.HorizontalScope())
{
    //Draw the buttons
}
```

Layout Options

Next, you can specify a height and width for most GUILayout calls by passing a GUILayoutOption to the corresponding method. In Listing 3-7, you pass a GUILayout.Height to the GUILayout.Button method to make it taller. This button will toggle the active state of all GameObjects that have the EnemyBehaviour. You can see the new button in Figure 3-17.

Listing 3-7. Passing in a GUILayout.Height Option to the Button

```
if (GUILayout.Button("Disable/Enable all enemy", GUILayout.
Height(40)))
{
        foreach (var enemy in GameObject.FindObjectsOfType<Enem
        yBehaviour>(true))
        {
enemy.gameObject.SetActive(!enemy.gameObject.activeSelf);
        }
}
```

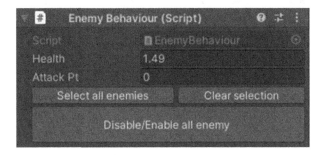

Figure 3-17. *After adding the button with height = 40*

You can also limit the width by passing in GUILayout.Width(40).

Coloring the Button

With the button you just created, you can emphasize this action with color (Figure 3-18) by temporarily setting the GUI.background color and reverting the color value back when the GUI has been drawn (Listing 3-8).

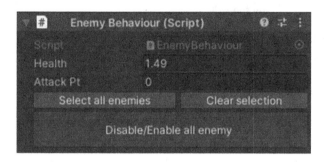

Figure 3-18. *Colored button*

Listing 3-8. Coloring the Button Background by Setting GUI. backgroundColor

```
var cachedColor = GUI.backgroundColor;
GUI.backgroundColor = Color.green;
// The button's code
GUI.backgroundColor = cachedColor;
```

This is an easy way to highlight any part of the UI with a specific color tint. According to the official code comment of the GUI class, you can also change the GUI.color or GUI.contentColor for more precise coloring. See Table 3-1.

45

Table 3-1. *Available Static Fields in the GUI Class for Color*

Field	Description
color	Global tinting color for the GUI
backgroundColor	Global tinting color for all background elements rendered by the GUI
contentColor	Tinting color for all text rendered by the GUI

Custom Undo/Redo

When you click the "Disable/Enable all enemy" button, you might be unable to undo after setting the GameObjects' active state. This is because you didn't handle the undo properly. In this case of setting the active state, you must use the Undo class in UnityEditor to instruct the undo system to record the Unity object you are going to be modifying.

You just need a line of code, Undo.RecordObject, that tells Unity to keep a copy of the Unity object that you are going to modify. By passing in a name describing your action (Listing 3-9), it will appear as a normal undo action in the undo menu item (Figure 3-19).

Listing 3-9. Recording a Undoable Operation

```
foreach (var enemy in GameObject.FindObjectsOfType
<EnemyBehaviour>(true))
{
    Undo.RecordObject(enemy.gameObject, "Disable/Enable
    enemy");
    enemy.gameObject.SetActive(!enemy.gameObject.activeSelf);
}
```

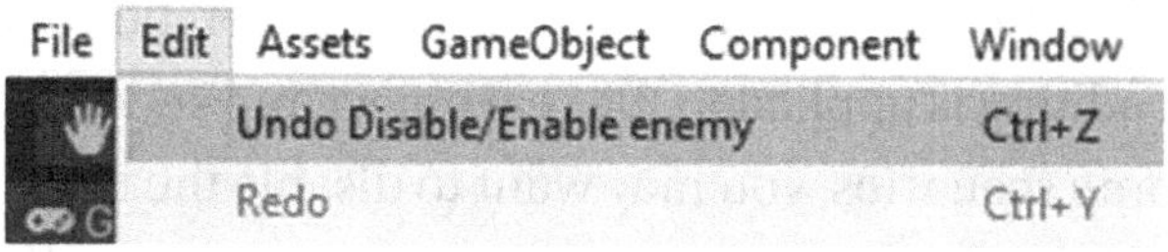

Figure 3-19. *Undo record showing in the menu*

Drawing the Property Field Yourself

Remember the `base.OnInspectorGUI()` method call that renders the default GUI? In order to be more flexible with the custom editor, you can draw those fields yourself. For instance, you may want to display a `HelpBox` warning the user that some input is not valid, so you need to control the draw order of the inspector.

Since you will be handling the component field's GUI instead of letting the default inspector draw itself, you must know about the `serializedObject` provided in the `Editor` class. A `SerializedObject` is like a middleman handling data editing for Unity objects. It is automatically created by the `Editor` class for the editing objects and makes it easier to support the undo operation and GUI drawing. With the combination of the `EditorGUILayout.PropertyField,` you can easily draw the GUI that properly displays the type of field like the default inspector by passing in the corresponding `PropertyField` contained in the `serializedObject`. Using the code in Listing 3-10, you can draw the property field identically to the default inspector.

Listing 3-10. Drawing a Field GUI with PropertyField

```
serializedObject.Update();

var health = serializedObject.FindProperty("health");
var attackPt = serializedObject.FindProperty("attackPt");

EditorGUILayout.PropertyField(health);
EditorGUILayout.PropertyField(attackPt);

serializedObject.ApplyModifiedProperties();
```

47

ApplyModifiedProperties is where the undo operation is registered when the data editing is applied to the real object and serialized to disk. However, in some scenarios, you may want to disable the undo operation. You can do that by calling ApplyModifiedPropertiesWithoutUndo() instead. See Figure 3-20.

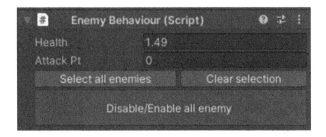

Figure 3-20. *Result of drawing the field GUI with PropertyField*

Note   A side effect of drawing the field GUI yourself is that the script reference field is gone, which could be useful to make more space for the rest of the GUI. Alternatively, to hide the reference field without drawing PropertyField one by one, use DrawPropertiesExclu ding(serializedObject, "m_Script");.

Without using the PropertyField, you can directly draw the type of the control you want. For instance, you can draw a slider yourself for the health field using the Slider method in the EditorGUILayout class (Listing 3-11).

Listing 3-11. Method Definition of the Slider Method in the EditorGUILayout Class

```
public static float Slider(float value, float leftValue, float
rightValue, params GUILayoutOption[] options);
```

However, you will need to handle more stuff yourself. Listing 3-12 shows a sample. First, you need to wrap a ChangeCheckScope to see if the GUI was changed, and only update the value of the SerializedProperty health when its changed. For most of the GUI you see in Unity Editor, you can find a way to draw it with IMGUI somehow. The best way is to look through the documentation and Unity's C# Reference[2].

Listing 3-12. Drawing a Slider GUI Without Using a RangeAttribute

```
using (var changeScope = new EditorGUI.ChangeCheckScope())
{
    var temp = EditorGUILayout.Slider("Health", health.
    floatValue, 0, 10);
    if (changeScope.changed)
    {
        health.floatValue = temp;
    }
}
```

Getting a Value in SerializedProperty

With the serializedObject.FindProperty method you were able to find and reference a SerializedProperty that represents the serializable field in your component and holds the temporary value of the editing field. It is "generic" in the way that a SerializedProperty can hold the value of most serializable types (e.g. bool, float, string). To access the correct type of field, you have to get the correct value property (Figure 3-21) and be sure that you are getting the correct type of the actual field in your class. For example, to get the float value from the health property, you use health. floatValue since it is a float field.

For custom types, which could be your custom serializable class and nested fields, it is also supported by the SerializedProperty. I will go through this in the later part of the chapter when I talk about custom serializable classes.

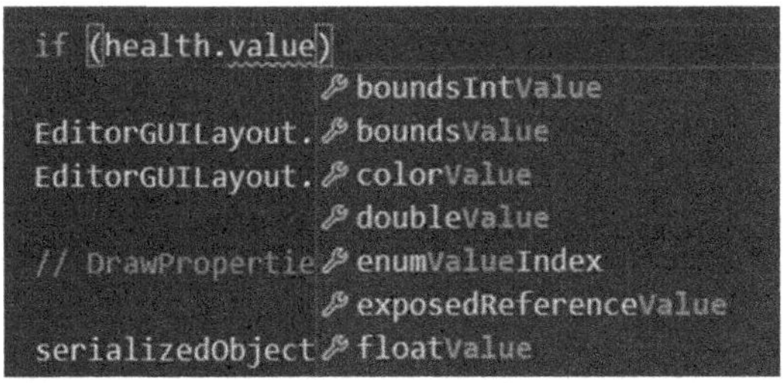

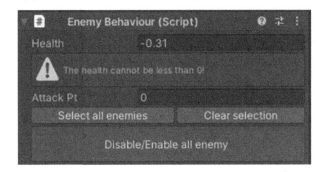

Figure 3-21. *Different value types in a SerializedProperty*

HelpBox

So, now that you know how to retrieve the value for the editing field via the SerializedProperty for your health property, let's display a warning with a HelpBox when the health is less than 0 (Figure 3-22). The first argument you pass in for the EditorGUILayout.HelpBox is the message to display (Listing 3-13), while the second one decides which type the message is and this affects which icon is shown (Table 3-2). HelpBox is useful for displaying any kind of important message to the user with your custom inspector.

Figure 3-22. *Warning HelpBox in the inspector*

Listing 3-13. Showing a HelpBox When the Health Is Negative

```
if (health.floatValue < 0)
{
    EditorGUILayout.HelpBox("...", MessageType.Warning);
}
```

Table 3-2. *HelpBox MessageType and Corresponding Display*

MessageType	Result
None	The health cannot be less than 0!
Info	The health cannot be less than 0!
Warning	The health cannot be less than 0!
Error	The health cannot be less than 0!

Property Drawers

Creating a custom inspector GUI is cool, but what if you have a bunch of components and creating a custom inspector class for each of them is time consuming? You are in luck because Unity has a `PropertyDrawer` class which has two main purposes:

- It draw a custom GUI for a script member that has custom attribute.

- It draws a custom GUI for a script member that is a custom `Serializable` class.

Simply put, you can create a custom PropertyAttribute, like RangeAttribute, HeaderAttribute, or TextAreaAttribute mentioned in the previous chapter, which means you can then reuse the custom GUI code easily without creating a custom editor. Moreover, if you have a custom data class, for example a DialogueEntry class, possibly containing a string representing the character name and a string for the actual content, then it can be marked as SerializableAttribute, and with PropertyDrawer, you can define a custom GUI for this class, and wherever you used this class in a MonoBehaviour or ScriptableObject, the custom GUI will be rendered instead of the default one.

Custom Property Attribute

Similar to RangeAttribute, PropertyAttributes allows you create a custom attribute to override the GUI drawing for that script member in the inspector. To make it easier for you to grasp the concept of a custom PropertyAttribute, you will create a custom FloatPickerAttribute. The idea is to define a list of floats in the attribute to let the user quickly select a preset value for the float field in the editor. First, you create the component you are going to utilize with the custom FloatPickerAttribute. Name the file FloatPicker.cs (Listing 3-14). It has a float field with a FloatPickerAttribute that you are going to create next.

Listing 3-14. FloatPicker Component

```
using UnityEngine;
public class FloatPicker : MonoBehaviour
{
    [FloatPicker(options = new float[] { 10, 20, 30 })]
    public float someFloat;
}
```

Next, you create the Attribute class in the same file by extending PropertyAttribute and creating a float array called options to store a list of floats for the float picker. See Listing 3-15.

Listing 3-15. FloatPickerAttribute

```
public class FloatPickerAttribute : PropertyAttribute
{
    public float[] options;
}
```

Note   If the class name for the Attribute class has a suffix of "Attribute" like FloatPickerAttribute (Listing 3-15), the compiler allow you to omit it when using it, like [FloatPicker(...)], as shown in Listing 3-14.

Now, to create the actual custom PropertyDrawer that is going to draw the GUI, first you include the UnityEditor namespace using statement at the top of the file and then you create the FloatPickerAttributeDrawer class by extending from PropertyDrawer. By adding the CustomPropertyDrawerAttribute to the drawer class, you can associate this drawer with a type, so Unity knows what type of drawer is responsible for drawing the GUI. See Listing 3-16.

Listing 3-16. A Custom PropertyDrawer

```
#if UNITY_EDITOR
using UnityEditor;
#endif

#if UNITY_EDITOR
[CustomPropertyDrawer(typeof(FloatPickerAttribute))]
```

```
public class FloatPickerAttributeDrawer : PropertyDrawer
{
    public override void OnGUI(Rect position,
    SerializedProperty property, GUIContent label)
    {
        var attr = (FloatPickerAttribute)attribute;

        EditorGUI.BeginProperty(position, label, property);

        // Core GUI code here

        EditorGUI.EndProperty();
    }
}
#endif
```

Now for the actual GUI part. When doing a GUI in the PropertyDrawer, you must handle the layout calculation yourself, therefore you cannot use EditorGUILayout. Instead, you use EditorGUI. However, it's not that hard. First, you calculate the main property's Rect size from position (which is the size and position rect of the current drawing property), minus its width by 20 units to make some room for the dropdown button. Next, you calculate the dropdownButtonRect by setting the start position to the xMax of the propertyRect directly and its width to 20 units. See Listing 3-17.

Listing 3-17. Calculating the Rect Size for Your Main Property and the Dropdown Button

```
var propertyRect = new Rect(position.x, position.y, position.
width - 20, position.height);
        var dropdownButtonRect = new Rect(propertyRect.xMax,
        position.y, 20, position.height);
```

After the Rect size, you can start drawing the float field GUI by calling the EditorGUI.PropertyField (Listing 3-18), instead of EditorGUILayout, since you are calculating the GUI size yourself, and you need to pass in propertyRect and the property (which is the current drawing property) to it.

Listing 3-18. Drawing PropertyField with EditorGUI

```
EditorGUI.PropertyField(propertyRect, property);
```

For the button, you use GUI.Button instead of GUILayout.Button. Then you pass in the dropdownButtonRect and the name for the button. When the button is pressed, you create a new GenericMenu. This is a way to display a menu with a list of items and individual selected callbacks. Next, you do a simple foreach loop for the options array in the attr, which is the FloatPickerAttribute you created earlier. Then you can set the property's float value to the selected option value and invoke the ApplyModifiedProperties method to make sure the changes are recorded. See Listing 3-19.

Listing 3-19. Drawing the Button That Will Show the Popup Menu

```
if (GUI.Button(dropdownButtonRect, "..."))
{
    var menu = new GenericMenu();
    foreach (var option in attr.options)
    {
        menu.AddItem(new GUIContent(option.ToString()), false,
        () =>
        {
            // set the property value to selected
            property.floatValue = option;
            // Apply the modified values
            property.serializedObject.ApplyModifiedProperties();
```

```
        });
    }
    menu.ShowAsContext();
}
```

Your `FloatPicker` component will look like Figure 3-23. You can reuse your `FloatPickerAttribute` anywhere.

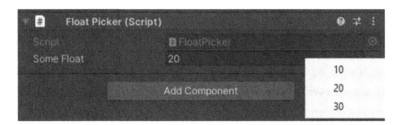

Figure 3-23. *Result of the FloatPickerAttribute custom drawer*

Note   To create custom decoration-only drawers that will not override the original GUI of the property, extend from `DecoratorDrawer` instead of `PropertyDrawer`, like the `Space` or `Header` attribute, they are only for decoration purposes. Useful situation will be drawing a custom separator.

Custom Serializable Class

Another powerful feature is that with a custom class that is Serializable you can define a custom GUI for it in Unity, such as the `DialogueEntry` class mentioned above. Say you want to store an array of `DialogueEntry`s representing the whole dialogue's data. You can create a `DialogueBehaviour.cs` script containing all the classes in this example (Listing 3-20). For the `DialogueEntry` class, make sure to add the `SerializableAttribute` from the `System` namespace so that it can be serialized and exposed in the inspector.

Listing 3-20. DialogueBehaviour Component and a DialogueEntry
Class

```
using UnityEngine;

public class DialogueBehaviour : MonoBehaviour
{
    public DialogueEntry[] dialogues;
}

[System.Serializable]
public class DialogueEntry
{
    public string character;
    public string content;
}
```

Without a custom GUI for the DialogueEntry class, the default
property GUI will be used for classes and a foldout will be shown to expand
the class properties (Figure 3-24), which might take up a lot of space in the
inspector and is not intuitive to use.

Figure 3-24. *Default GUI for serializable custom class*

Note   Since Unity 2020.2, the array and list will be reorderable by default in the editor. To disable a reorderable GUI, add NonReorderableAttrribute to the array or list.

Now, let's create a custom PropertyDrawer (Listing 3-21) to streamline the DialogueEntry's GUI, which shows the two fields side by side. First, you add in using a namespace for the UnityEditor at the top of the file. Then you create the DialogueEntryDrawer class extending PropertyDrawer with the CustomPropertyDrawerAttribute passing in the type of the DialogueEntry class. Next, you override the GetPropertyHeight method of the PropertyDrawer so that you can ensure a large height area for drawing the GUI.

Listing 3-21. DialogueEntryDrawer Class

```
#if UNITY_EDITOR
using UnityEditor;
#endif

#if UNITY_EDITOR
[CustomPropertyDrawer(typeof(DialogueEntry))]
public class DialogueEntryDrawer : PropertyDrawer
{
    public override float GetPropertyHeight(SerializedProperty
    property, GUIContent label)
    {
        return EditorGUIUtility.singleLineHeight * 2;
    }

    public override void OnGUI(Rect position,
    SerializedProperty property, GUIContent label)
    {
```

```
        EditorGUI.BeginProperty(position, label, property);

        // Core GUI code here

        EditorGUI.EndProperty();
    }
}
#endif
```

The core GUI code (Listing 3-22) is straightforward. First, you calculate the rects. Then you do an EditorGUI.PropertyField call. Since this is not a single string or float property (it's a class with nested properties), you must look for the relative property by property.FindPropertyRelative and pass into the PropertyField method. You must also pass in GUIContent.none at the second argument so the label of the property is not drawn. Now the result is much more intuitive to use (Figure 3-25) and you can add in new dialogue lines easily without having to expand or collapse the foldout in the default GUI.

Listing 3-22. Calculating the Rects and Drawing the Properties

```
var characterRect = new Rect(position.x, position.y, 100,
position.height);
var contentRect = new Rect(characterRect.xMax, position.y,
position.width - characterRect.width, position.height);

EditorGUI.PropertyField(characterRect, property.FindPropertyRel
ative("character"), GUIContent.none);
EditorGUI.PropertyField(contentRect, property.FindPropertyRelat
ive("content"), GUIContent.none);
```

Figure 3-25. *Customized DialogueEntry GUI with PropertyDrawer*

Custom Editor Window

Now that you know how to create a custom `Editor` class for your
components and a custom `PropertyDrawer` for attributes and serializable
classes, let's talk about `EditorWindow`, which let the user dock anywhere
inside Unity Editor or acts as a standalone window. In the following
example, you are going to create a little helper window that is going to
help you load different scenes in the project. The idea is to create a simple
editor window that will list all the scenes found in the project build settings
and can load them directly or additively.

Extending EditorWindow

Let's create a new editor script, `LevelEditorWindow.` Since this time it's
more editor-focused, you can just place it inside your `Editor` folder. See
Figure 3-26.

Figure 3-26. *Placing the LevelEditorWindow class in the Editor*
folder

Inside the script, let's create the LevelEditorWindow class and extend from UnityEditor.EditorWindow, create an OnGUI method, and a private static method that shows the editor window and is marked with a MenuItem attribute (Listing 3-23).

Listing 3-23. LevelEditorWindow Class

```
using UnityEngine;
using UnityEditor;

public class LevelEditorWindow : EditorWindow
{
    [MenuItem("Window/LevelWindow")]
    private static void ShowWindow()
    {
        var window = GetWindow<LevelEditorWindow>();
        window.titleContent = new GUIContent("LevelWindow");
        window.Show();
    }

    private void OnGUI()
    {
        //...
    }
}
```

With the MenuItem attribute on the static method, a menu item will display in the relative path, and the method will be called when the menu is clicked. See Figure 3-27.

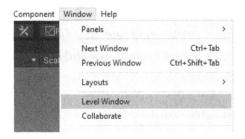

Figure 3-27. *The menu item to open the editor*

If you click the menu item, you will see the window show up! You may want to set a `minSize` for the `EditorWindow`. In this case, the size is very small on startup. See Listing 3-24.

Listing 3-24. Setting the minSize When the Editor Is Being Enabled

```
private void OnEnable()
{
    minSize = new Vector2(300, 100);
}
```

Now, on to the GUI part. Figure 3-28 shows what you are trying to build in this example. There will be a toolbar at the top and a list of scenes with the button to load it. First, you split the drawing code into two methods, `DrawToolbar` and `DrawSceneList,` to handle both parts. See Listing 3-25.

Listing 3-25. Main OnGUI Method

```
private void OnGUI()
{
    DrawToolbar();
    DrawSceneList();
}
```

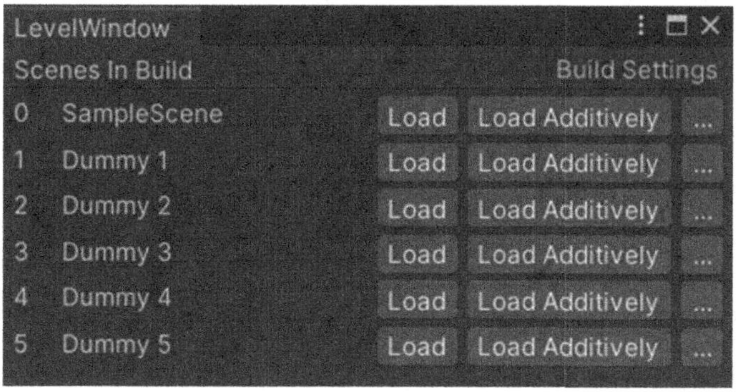

Figure 3-28. *The LevelEditorWindow you are going to build*

The DrawToolbar method in Listing 3-26 is of a horizontal layout with the toolbar styles from the EditorStyles class (an editor class that contains most editor styles for IMGUI). Inside the toolbar, there will be a simple GUILayout.Label for the title followed with a flexible space to expand the layout and fill in the empty space. Lastly, you'll have a simple GUILayout.Button with the EditorStyles.toolbarButton style and it will trigger the menu item to open the build settings window when clicked.

Listing 3-26. DrawToolbar Method

```
private void DrawToolbar()
{
    using (new EditorGUILayout.HorizontalScope(EditorStyles.
    toolbar))
    {
        GUILayout.Label("Scenes In Build");
        GUILayout.FlexibleSpace();
        if (GUILayout.Button("Build Settings", EditorStyles.
        toolbarButton))
```

```
        {
            EditorApplication.ExecuteMenuItem("File/Build
            Settings...");
        }
    }
}
```

For the DrawSceneList method, you wrap the whole layout into a
ScrollView (Listing 3-27), and then loop through the scenes from the
EditorBuildSettings to draw the list item for each of the scenes. Since the
IMGUI is a stateless mode, you must cache the ScrollView's scroll position
to preserve the scrolling state. Therefore, you also need to add a private
field to store the scrollPosition from the ScrollViewScope.

Listing 3-27. DrawSceneList Method

```
private Vector2 scrollPosition;

private void DrawSceneList()
{
    //Drawing the scroll view
    using (var scrollViewScope = new EditorGUILayout.ScrollView
    Scope(scrollPosition))
    {
        scrollPosition = scrollViewScope.scrollPosition;
        for (int i = 0; i < EditorBuildSettings.scenes.Length;
        i++)
        {
            EditorBuildSettingsScene scene =
            EditorBuildSettings.scenes[i];
            DrawSceneListItem(i, scene);
        }
    }
}
```

To draw the scene list item (Figure 3-29), you separate the logic into another method (Listing 3-28).

Figure 3-29. *Drawing the scene item's index and title*

Listing 3-28. DrawSceneListItem Method

```
private void DrawSceneListItem(int i, EditorBuildSettingsScene
scene)
{
    var sceneName = Path.GetFileNameWithoutExtension(scene.
    path);
    using (new EditorGUILayout.HorizontalScope())
    {
        GUILayout.Label(i.ToString(), GUILayout.Width(20));
        GUILayout.Label(new GUIContent(sceneName, scene.path));
        GUILayout.FlexibleSpace();

        // Buttons...
    }
}
```

Lastly, you draw the three buttons to load a scene (Figure 3-30), load a scene additively, and show a generic menu (Figure 3-31) to ping the scene asset in the project window (Listing 3-29).

Figure 3-30. *Drawing the buttons after the title*

65

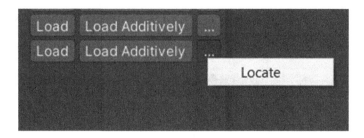

Figure 3-31. *GenericMenu when clicking the third button*

Listing 3-29. Drawing the Buttons

```
if (GUILayout.Button("Load"))
{
    if (EditorSceneManager.
    SaveCurrentModifiedScenesIfUserWantsTo())
        EditorSceneManager.OpenScene(scene.path);
}
if (GUILayout.Button("Load Additively"))
{
    if (EditorSceneManager.SaveCurrentModifiedScenes
    IfUserWantsTo())
        EditorSceneManager.OpenScene(scene.path, OpenSceneMode.
        Additive);
}
if (GUILayout.Button("..."))
{
    var menu = new GenericMenu();
    menu.AddItem(new GUIContent("Locate"), false, () =>
    {
        var sceneAsset = AssetDatabase.LoadAssetAtPath
        <SceneAsset>(scene.path);
```

```
        EditorGUIUtility.PingObject(sceneAsset);
    });
    menu.ShowAsContext();
}
```

GenericMenu

The third button, which uses a GenericMenu class, allows you to show a popup menu in Unity Editor like other system-level menus. Besides having multiple items like you did in the FloatPickerAttribute previously, there are more features to it. For instance, you can add a separator, you can disable items, and you can mark an item as selected by passing in true for the second argument (Figure 3-32). See Listing 3-30.

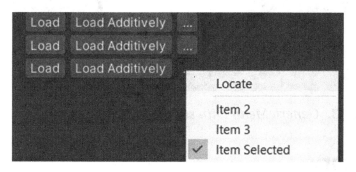

Figure 3-32. *Multiple items, separators, disabled items, and selected items in GenericMenu*

Listing 3-30. Adding Multiple Items, Separators, Disabled Items, and selected Items

```
menu.AddSeparator("");
menu.AddItem(new GUIContent("Item 2"), false, () => { });
menu.AddItem(new GUIContent("Item 3"), false, () => { });
menu.AddDisabledItem(new GUIContent("Item 4"));
menu.AddItem(new GUIContent("Item Selected"), true, () => { });
```

And even more powerful, you can use / to indicate a submenu path in Listing 3-31 (as shown in Figure 3-33).

Listing 3-31. Adding an Item with a Submenu Path

```
menu.AddItem(new GUIContent("Item 3/More item here"), false, ()
=> { });
menu.AddItem(new GUIContent("Item 3/More item here 2"), false,
() => { });
```

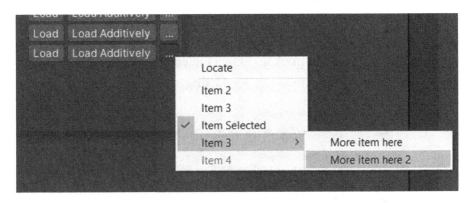

Figure 3-33. *GenericMenu with submenu items*

Summary

In this chapter, you learned about the difference between runtime scripts and editor scripts. You can place your editor scripts in a special folder named Editor. You can use the #if preprocessor to have your editor code in runtime scripts without build errors. With asmdef, you can increase code recompilation speed by separating your code into a separated Assembly. You can also leverage other advantages of asmdef. While the Editor folder, #if preprocessor, and asmdef can be used at the same time without conflicts, you also walked through how to create custom Editor, PropertyDrawer, and EditorWindow classes. The custom Editor and

`EditorWindow` examples used the `EditorGUILayout` and `GUILayout` class for IMGUI, while for the custom `PropertyDrawer` you use the `EditorGUI` and `GUI` classes to draw a manual calculated layout. You should now understand the concept of how custom editors can be implemented in Unity with IMGUI.

In the following chapter, I will introduce the UI Toolkit for Editor. You will create similar editor scripts as in this chapter but you will be using the UI Toolkit over IMGUI for custom `Editor`, `PropertyDrawer`, and `EditorWindow` classes.

CHAPTER 4

Custom Editor with UI Toolkit

The UI Toolkit is Unity's new retained-mode GUI solution to help with both editor GUI and runtime UI creation. At the time of writing, the UI Toolkit for runtime is still in preview and under active development. However, it is usable for editor GUI authoring and has many new features plus flexibility over IMGUI. In this chapter, I will walk you through the basic ways of creating an editor GUI with UI Toolkit by implementing a custom editor, PropertyDrawer, and EditorWindow with UI Toolkit via C# and UI Builder (the drag-and-drop UI builder for UI Toolkit).

Custom Editor with UI Toolkit via C#

You are going to create a new C# script called EnemyBehaviourUIToolkit and an editor class called EnemyBehaviourUIToolkitEditor that will mimic the custom editor GUI layout from the IMGUI chapter, but using UI Toolkit via C# instead. Look at Listing 4-1.

With UI Toolkit, you extend your custom editor from the Editor class, but instead of overriding the OnGUI method, you override the CreateInspectorGUI method and return a new VisualElement inside your custom editor class.

© Benny Kok 2021

B. Kok, *Beginning Unity Editor Scripting*, https://doi.org/10.1007/978-1-4842-7167-4_4

UI Toolkit was named UI Elements previously, and the namespace in C# will still remain UIElements for the near future. In UI Toolkit, everything is a VisualElement, and it uses a CSS-like styling called USS (Unity Style Sheets), which is similar to an HTML document. A VisualElement in UI Toolkit is like a div in HTML. Under the hood, the layout engine[1] uses the Yoga[2] open source project and implements a subset of Flexbox, which allows complex layout structuring defined by USS or inline styles with ease.

Listing 4-1. Custom Editor with UI Toolkit Using VisualElement

```
using UnityEngine;

#if UNITY_EDITOR
using UnityEngine.UIElements;
using UnityEditor.UIElements;
using UnityEditor;
#endif

public class EnemyBehaviourUIToolkit : MonoBehaviour
{
    public float health;
    public float attackPt;
}

#if UNITY_EDITOR
[CustomEditor(typeof(EnemyBehaviourUIToolkit)),
CanEditMultipleObjects]
public class EnemyBehaviourUIToolkitEditor : Editor
{
```

---

[1]https://docs.unity3d.com/Manual/UIE-LayoutEngine.html
[2]https://github.com/facebook/yoga

```
public override VisualElement CreateInspectorGUI()
{
    var container = new VisualElement();

    // Code to create VisualElement and add to the container.

    return container;
}
}
#endif
```

Displaying a Button

Now let's try displaying a simple button by creating a `Button`
`VisualElement` and simply adding it to the container so that it can be
rendered (Figure 4-1). See Listing 4-2.

Listing 4-2. Creating and Adding a Button VisualElement to the
Layout

```
container.Add(new Button()
{
    text = "Button in UI Toolkit!"
});
```

With C#, you can do a member assignment by using a bracket after
the new statement. It's called the **object initializer**, which in this case
makes it way easier to apply the styling and setting properties to each
`VisualElement` created in code.

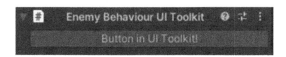

Figure 4-1. A custom button in the inspector with UI Toolkit

Detecting a Button Click

Next, to receive a button click callback from the event system of UI Toolkit, you can simply pass in a lambda expression to the constructor of the Button class (Listing 4-3). When testing the button click, you will see the log in the console (Figure 4-2).

Listing 4-3. Creating and Adding a Button VisualElement with an On-Click Callback

```
container.Add(new Button(() =>
{
    Debug.Log("I'm clicked!");
})
{
    text = "Button in UI Toolkit!"
});
```

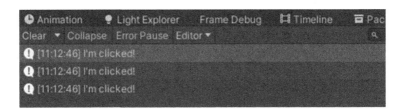

Figure 4-2. *The Debug.Log result when clicking on the button*

To clear up confusion, an alternative way to Listing 4-3, without inlining the code, is shown in Listing 4-4. Adding the lambda to the clicked action directly produces the same result.

Listing 4-4. Alternative Way to Listing 4-3

```
var myButton = new Button();
myButton.clicked += () =>
{
    Debug.Log("I'm clicked!");
};
myButton.text = "Button in UI Toolkit!";
container.Add(myButton);
```

Inline Styling in Code

If you have **Visual Studio Code** set up correctly, you should be seeing all of the styling suggestions when you assign the `style` property for the button you just created (see Figure 4-3). You can explore all of the available styling options. Let's try some basic styling with this button.

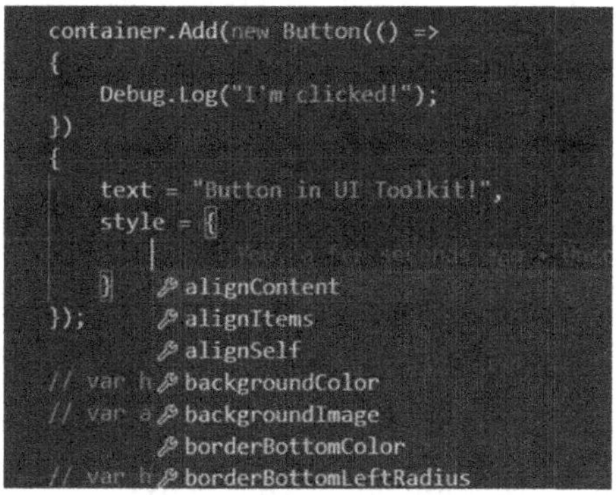

Figure 4-3. The style suggestions with intelliSense in VS code

By assigning the `style` property, you can set inline styles to any `VisualElement`-derived class directly. Let's will look into various common styling options.

First, you can set the height of the button to a fixed value and assign a text color for it (Listing 4-5). The result is shown in Figure 4-4.

Listing 4-5. Style with 60-Unit Height and Cyan as the Color

```
style = {
    height = 60,
    color = Color.cyan
}
```

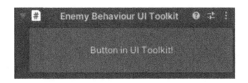

Figure 4-4. *The result of the styled button*

Next, let's talk about modifying the font and text styles. You can set the fontSize to a fixed value, unityTextAlign for the text alignment, and unityFontStyleAndWeight for bold, italic, or normal (see Listing 4-6). The results are shown in Figure 4-5.

Listing 4-6. Style with Text Align and a Bold Font

```
style = {
    height = 60,
    fontSize = 20,
    unityTextAlign = TextAnchor.MiddleLeft,
    unityFontStyleAndWeight = FontStyle.Bold
}
```

Figure 4-5. *The result of the styled button with a bold and left-aligned text label*

Next, you can utilize the `alignSelf` property to align specific items (Listing 4-7). For example, you can set the button to `Align.FlexStart`, which will align the button at the start of the layout, as shown in Figure 4-6.

Listing 4-7. Style with Self-Align to the Start of the Flex Layout

```
style = {
    alignSelf = Align.FlexStart
}
```

Figure 4-6. *The result of the styled button with self-align*

Now that you have the basic concept of how a button can be created and styled with C# in the UI Toolkit, let's explore ways to lay out your GUI.

UI Toolkit Debugger

Now onto the interesting part! With UI Toolkit, you get a Google Chrome-like inspector experience in Unity for all of the `VisualElements` in the editor with **UI Toolkit Debugger.**

In any editor window, the top right context menu (the three-dots drop down) will show the UI Toolkit Debugger options. Open it directly (Figure 4-7), or press Ctrl + F5 to open it up.

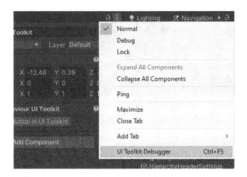

Figure 4-7. *The menu item to open the UI Toolkit Debugger*

You can see the `VisualElements`' hierarchy and their style attributes (Figure 4-8).

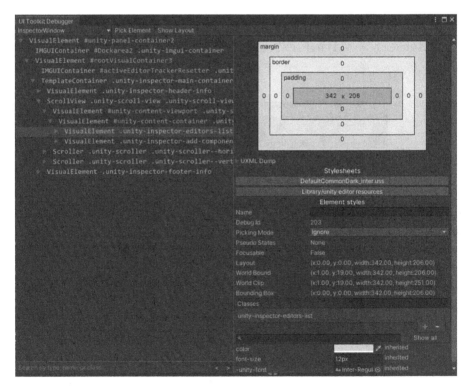

Figure 4-8. *UI Toolkit Debugger*

Now let's inspect the button you just created by clicking the "Pick Element" button in the toolbar and then hovering over the inspector of your GameObject. It will be highlighted in blue (Figure 4-9). Once you click it, it will be selected in the debugger window (Figure 4-10) and will show you all the styles of this VisualElement.

Figure 4-9. *Selecting your VisualElement in the inspector*

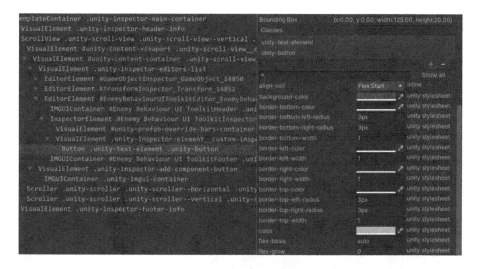

Figure 4-10. *UI Toolkit Debugger with the selected element*

It's possible to preview and change the color (Figure 4-11) and all other styles in real time, allowing you to debug and try out different attributes right in the editor.

Figure 4-11. *Changing the color of the button in UI Toolkit Debugger*

UI Toolkit Samples

UI Toolkit comes with a samples editor window showcasing all the possible GUI control style examples (Figure 4-12). You can find it in at Window > UI Toolkit > Samples.

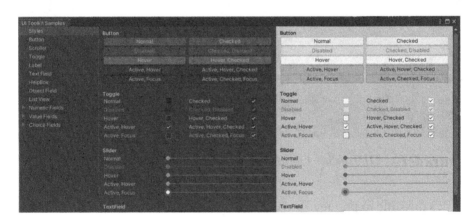

Figure 4-12. *UI Toolkit Samples*

The UI Toolkit Samples window also comes with code examples for creating the VisualElement in C# or with UXML (Figure 4-13). It's great if you want to look up specific code examples.

Figure 4-13. *UI Toolkit Samples with code examples*

Layout in UI Toolkit

Now, back to the custom editor. As mentioned in the chapter about IMGUI, to create a horizontal layout, you use the BeginHorizontal method for a horizontal layout. For a vertical layout, you use the BeginVertical method. With UI Toolkit, you need to create a parent VisualElement with its style set to FlexDirection.Row for a horizontal layout or FlexDirection.Column for a vertical layout. The children will be placed automatically along the direction. Let's try with a row first (Listing 4-8).

Listing 4-8. Creating a Row VisualElement

```
var row = new VisualElement()
{
    style = {
        flexDirection = FlexDirection.Row,
    }
};
```

Next, you create two buttons (Listing 4-9) and add them to the row VisualElement above, so the layout engine will place them side by side. By setting the flexGrow value of each button, it acts as a weighting to the elements[3]. The larger the value, the larger the flexible space it is going to take up. By setting each to 1, they take up the same amount of flexible space (Figure 4-14).

Listing 4-9. Creating and Adding Buttons to the Row

```
row.Add(new Button()
{
    text = "Select all enemies",
    style = { flexGrow = 1 }
});
row.Add(new Button()
{
    text = "Clear selection",
    style = { flexGrow = 1 }
});
```

Finally adding the row to the container,

```
container.Add(row);
```

---

[3]https://docs.unity3d.com/Manual/UIE-LayoutEngine.html

Figure 4-14. *VisualElement parent with row flexDirection*

Different flexGrow values, such as setting the first button to a value of 2 (Listing 4-10), will produce the result shown in Figure 4-15.

Listing 4-10. Trying Different flexGrow Values for the Buttons

```
row.Add(new Button()
{
    text = "Select all enemies",
    style = { flexGrow = 2 }
});
row.Add(new Button()
{
    text = "Clear selection",
    style = { flexGrow = 1 }
});
```

Figure 4-15. *VisualElement children with different flexGrow values*

Justify-Content

I highly recommend playing around with the justify-content attribute in the UI Toolkit Debugger (Figure 4-16). You don't have to wait for it to recompile if you decide to change it from the code (Listing 4-11) just to see the result.

When the children's `flexGrow` is set to 0, they warp around their contents. With the `justify-content` attribute, you can align the children in different ways for your `row` `VisualElement` (Figure 4-17 through Figure 4-21).

Figure 4-16.   *Changing justify-content in the UI Toolkit Debugger*

Listing 4-11.   Setting to Justify.Center from C#

```
style = {
    flexDirection = FlexDirection.Row,
    justifyContent = Justify.Center
}
```

Figure 4-17.   *VisualElement children 0 flexGrow value with default justifyContent = Flex.Start*

Figure 4-18.   *VisualElement parent with Justify.Center*

Figure 4-19. *VisualElement parent with Justify.SpaceBetween*

Figure 4-20. *VisualElement parent with Justify.FlexEnd*

Figure 4-21. *VisualElement parent with Justify.SpaceAround*

Property Field

Now that you know how to create horizontal and vertical layouts and customize them with simple inline styles via code, let's try adding the property field for your EnemyBehaviourUIToolkit script by using the PropertyField class in the UIElements namespace. It automatically handles the undo and serialization of the changes. See Listing 4-12.

Listing 4-12. Getting a Reference to the SerializedProperty and Creating a PropertyField

```
var health = serializedObject.FindProperty("health");
var attackPt = serializedObject.FindProperty("attackPt");

var healthPropField = new PropertyField(health);
var attackPtPropField = new PropertyField(attackPt);
```

Note   `PropertyField` here is also a `VisualElement`.

Next, to displaying them, you can add them to your container. See Listing 4-13. The result is shown in Figure 4-22.

Listing 4-13.   Adding the PropertyFields to the Container Before the Button Is Added

```
container.Add(healthPropField);
container.Add(attackPtPropField);
```

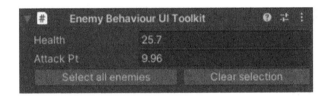

Figure 4-22.   *Result of using the PropertyField*

HelpBox

Oh, what about the `HelpBox` in the UI Toolkit? It also derives from `VisualElement`. You simply create a new `HelpBox` instance and pass in the message and message type (Listing 4-14).

Listing 4-14.   Creating a HelpBox VisualElement

```
var warningHelpBox = new HelpBox("The health cannot be less
than 0!", HelpBoxMessageType.Warning);
container.Add(warningHelpBox);
```

Note   The message type here in UI Toolkit is
`HelpBoxMessageType`. It is a different Enum type than the
`MessageType` used in the IMGUI help box.

The order you add to the layout also affects the order in the rendering
hierarchy (Figure 4-23). Since you want to display the warning `HelpBox`
underneath your health field, you arrange the add order as shown in
Listing 4-15.

Listing 4-15. Inserting the HelpBox After the Health PropertyField

```
container.Add(healthPropField);
container.Add(warningHelpBox);
container.Add(attackPtPropField);
```

Figure 4-23. *Result of adding the HelpBox to the layout*

Value Change Callback

Now you have a `HelpBox` that is always showing. In the previous IMGUI
example, you were able to check for the value in each render call. However,
in UI Toolkit, now you need to register a callback to the `PropertyField` and
it will notify you if there are changes in the value, so that you can toggle the
visibility of the `HelpBox`.

First, you create a method that takes in a SerializedProperty
(Listing 4-16) and a HelpBox and does the logic that decides if you want to
show the HelpBox by toggling the style.display between None and
Flex. (Flex is the default value.)

Listing 4-16. Creating a Separate Method to Toggle the HelpBox
Visibility

```
private void ShowWarningIfNeeded(SerializedProperty property,
HelpBox helpBox)
{
    helpBox.style.display = property.floatValue < 0 ?
    DisplayStyle.Flex : DisplayStyle.None;
}
```

Then you go back to the CreateInspectorGUI method and register the
value callback to the healthPropField (Listing 4-17). You also call the
method once when creating the GUI to make sure the initial display state
of the HelpBox is correct.

Listing 4-17. Hooking the Method to the Value Change Callback of
the Health PropertyField

```
// Calling the method once to correctly toggle the style on
first run
ShowWarningIfNeeded(health, warningHelpBox);
// Hooking the method to the value change callback
healthPropField.RegisterValueChangeCallback((e) =>
{
    ShowWarningIfNeeded(e.changedProperty, warningHelpBox);
});
```

Note   The value change callback will require a SerializedProperty ChangeEvent parameter for the lambda, and this class contains the changedProperty that references your health SerializedProperty. Therefore, you can use it to pass into your ShowWarningIfNeeded method.

Final Layout

With all the code together, you will get a complete workable GUI with VisualElement in UI Toolkit via C# (Figure 4-24).

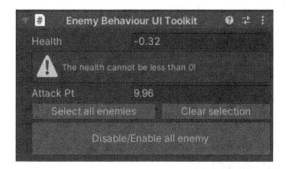

Figure 4-24. *The final layout of the custom editor with UI Toolkit*

Custom PropertyDrawer with UI Toolkit via C#

Creating a custom PropertyDrawer with UI Toolkit is possible with the advantage that you don't need to calculate the layout size yourself, but there is a catch[4]. Since the default editor is still drawn with IMGUI under the hood, and a VisualElement cannot be drawn inside IMGUI, therefore

---

[4]https://forum.unity.com/threads/property-drawers.595369/

any custom UI Toolkit PropertyDrawer for an attribute or custom class will not show up in default editor at this moment. You will have to implement a custom editor for your target component.

Let's create the custom FloatPicker MonoBehaviour and attribute for UIToolkit (Listing 4-18).

Listing 4-18. Creating a Custom PropertyAttribute and a Dummy MonoBehaviour Using the Attribute

```
using UnityEngine;

#if UNITY_EDITOR
using UnityEngine.UIElements;
using UnityEditor.UIElements;
using UnityEditor;
#endif

public class FloatPickerUIToolkit : MonoBehaviour
{
    [FloatPickerUIToolkit(options = new float[] { 10, 20, 30
})]
    public float someFloat;
}

public class FloatPickerUIToolkitAttribute : PropertyAttribute
{
    public float[] options;
}
```

Note   In case you missed the previous chapter, if the class name for the attribute class has a suffix of "Attribute," like FloatPickerUIToolkitAttribute, the compiler allows you to omit it when using it, such as [FloatPickerUIToolkit(...)].

After creating the attribute and the component, you will have
to create a custom editor to render your component with UI Toolkit
(VisualElement) or your PropertyEditor created in the later part won't
render because the default editor for the component is still using IMGUI in
current version of Unity.

Let's create a custom editor and use VisualElement for the target
component (Listing 4-19). You override the CreateInspectorGUI method
to return a parent container (VisualElement). Next, you loop through
the SerializedProperty of the component and create a PropertyField
(VisualElement) for each property and add to the container.

Looping through the SerializedProperty of the component is a bit
tricky. You must get the first item from the serializedObject by calling
GetIterator. By checking NextVisible, it will point itself to the next item
or return false if it reached the end of all the items.

Finally, in the do while loop, you also check if the current property is
the m_Script field and disable it so that your custom UIToolkit inspector
looks the same as the default one, which got the disabled script file
reference in the first row of all custom components.

Listing 4-19. Creating a Custom Editor Using VisualElement

```
#if UNITY_EDITOR
[CustomEditor(typeof(FloatPickerUIToolkit))]
public class FloatPickerUIToolkitEditor : Editor
{
    public override VisualElement CreateInspectorGUI()
    {
        var container = new VisualElement();
        var property = serializedObject.GetIterator();
        if (property.NextVisible(true))
        {
            do
```

```
            {
                var propertyField = new PropertyField(property.
                Copy());
                if (property.propertyPath == "m_Script")
                propertyField.SetEnabled(false);

                container.Add(propertyField);
            }
            while (property.NextVisible(false));
        }
        return container;
    }
}
```

Note   Listing 4-8 is a workaround for using `PropertyDrawer` with
UIToolkit (`VisualElement`) in the current version of Unity. Once
newer versions of Unity support it natively, this workaround will not
be needed for newer versions.

To implement the actual `PropertyDrawer`, you create a simple parent
`VisualElement` with `FlexDirection.Row` wrapping a `FloatField` and the
popup menu button (Listing 4-20).

For the `FloatField`, you need to bind it manually to the property and
also add the style `unity-property-field__label` to the `FloatField` label
to make sure the width of the label matches the normal property field in
this situation. To get a reference to the `Label` in the `floatField`, you can
use the Q method to query your target `VisualElement` with a specific type.

The result is a similar `PropertyDrawer` as the one you made with
IMGUI in the previous chapter (Figure 4-25).

Listing 4-20. Creating the PropertyDrawer for the Attribute with
UIToolkit

```
[CustomPropertyDrawer(typeof(FloatPickerUIToolkitAttribute))]
public class FloatPickerUIToolkitAttributeDrawer :
PropertyDrawer
{
    public override VisualElement CreatePropertyGUI(Serialized
    Property property)
    {
        var attr = (FloatPickerUIToolkitAttribute)attribute;

        var container = new VisualElement();
        container.style.flexDirection = FlexDirection.Row;

        var floatField = new FloatField()
        {
            label = property.displayName,
            style = {
                flexGrow = 1,
            },
        };
        floatField.Q<Label>().AddToClassList("unity-property-
        field__label");
        floatField.BindProperty(property);
        container.Add(floatField);

        container.Add(new Button(() =>
        {
            var menu = new GenericMenu();
            foreach (var option in attr.options)
            {
```

```
            menu.AddItem(new GUIContent(option.ToString()),
            false, () =>
            {
                // set the property value to selected
                property.floatValue = option;

                // Apply the modified values
                property.serializedObject.
                ApplyModifiedProperties();
            });
        }
        menu.ShowAsContext();
    })
    {
        text = "..."
    });

    return container;
    }
}
#endif
```

Figure 4-25. *The final result of the FloatPicker with UI Toolkit*

Custom Editor Window with UI Toolkit via UI Builder

Now you can try building a custom EditorWindow with UI Toolkit and recreate the level editor from the previous IMGUI chapter. There is a UI Builder package designed to make UI authoring easier with a drag-and-drop interface and generating the actual UXML behind the scene, and you will make use of it in this example. First, you need to install the package from UPM (Figure 4-26).

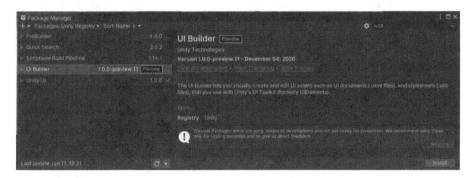

Figure 4-26. *Installing the UI Builder package*

After installing the UI Builder, in the project window, you can right-click and create a new UI Builder asset via Create > UI Toolkit > EditorWindow. As shown in Figure 4-27, name the C# and UXML file LevelEditorWindowUIToolkit and you can uncheck the USS generation in the creator window to keep it simple.

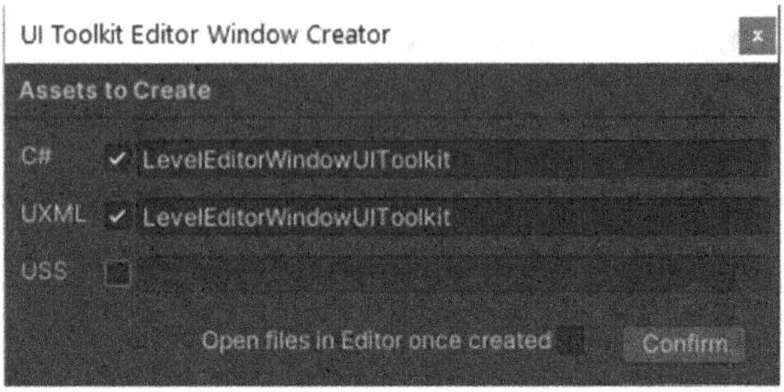

Figure 4-27. *Configuring the file to generate*

After generating the C# and UXML file, let's clean up the generated
LevelEditorWindowUIToolkit.cs file to remove the extra example code so
that it will only load the UXML layout into the rootVisualElement of the
EditorWindow (Listing 4-21).

Now, with UI Toolkit, you override the CreateGUI method to
handle the creation of the VisualElement in EditorWindow, and every
EditorWindow will contain the rootVisualElement that you will be
attaching your own VisualElement into it.

In this case, you are loading in the VisualElement from the UXML file,
and you use UI Builder to edit the layout in the next section.

Listing 4-21. Creating the Custom EditorWindow and Loading in
the UXML Layout

```
using System.IO;
using UnityEditor;
using UnityEditor.SceneManagement;
using UnityEngine;
using UnityEngine.UIElements;

public class LevelEditorWindowUIToolkit : EditorWindow
{
    [MenuItem("Window/Level Editor UI Toolkit")]
```

```
public static void ShowExample()
{
    LevelEditorWindowUIToolkit wnd = GetWindow<LevelEditor
    WindowUIToolkit>();
    wnd.titleContent = new GUIContent("LevelEditorWindow
    UIToolkit");
}

public void CreateGUI()
{
    VisualElement root = rootVisualElement;

    var visualTree = AssetDatabase.LoadAssetAtPath<Visual
    TreeAsset>("Assets/Editor/LevelEditorWindowUIToolkit.
    uxml");
    visualTree.CloneTree(root);

    // Initialize our ListView
}
}
```

Note   Keep in mind that you load the UXML with its file path, so if you moved your UXML file, you need to update the code to point to the correct path.

Now that you have everything set up, you can move on to creating the GUI with the UI Builder. To open the UI Builder (Figure 4-28), double-click the LevelEditorWindowUIToolkit.uxml file.

With the UI Builder open, there are different view areas for different functions. In the middle is the viewport, where you can view and position all the VisualElements in this document. On the right is the inspector, which shows the properties of the selected VisualElement. On the left are the style sheets, hierarchy, and library. The library panel shows the available VisualElements for you to drag and drop into the hierarchy or viewport.

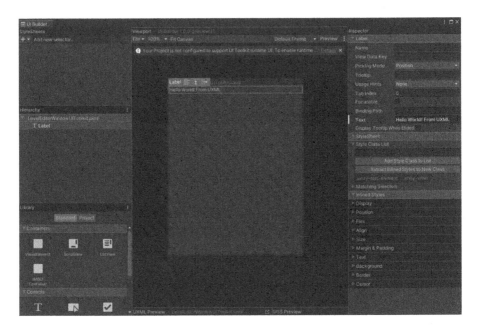

Figure 4-28. *UI Builder*

To create an editor-specific control, you must first enable the Editor Extension Authoring option in the option menu of the Library panel (Figure 4-29).

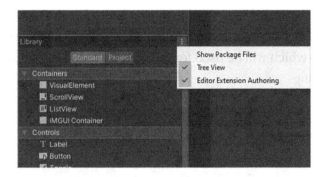

Figure 4-29.   *Toggle the options for the tree view display and the editor extension authoring*

Next, you can easily view the available runtime controls and editor-specific controls in the library panel. To recreate the toolbar element of your level editor, look for the toolbar control in the library panel, and drag and drop it into the viewport (Figure 4-30).

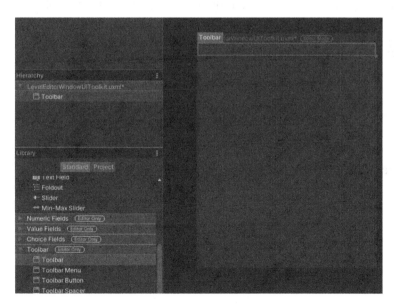

Figure 4-30.   *Creating a toolbar with UI Builder*

Next, drag in a label and ToolbarButton control to the hierarchy in the window above, to parent them under the toolbar control precisely (Figure 4-31), which will be used for the window title and button to open the build settings.

Figure 4-31. *Adding a label and ToolbarButton under the Toolbar*

For the label control, update the Text property over at the inspector to "Scenes In Build" and the ToolbarButton's text to "Build Settings." By setting the toolbar's Justify-Content to space-between, the second-to-last option (Figure 4-32), you get the result shown in Figure 4-33.

Figure 4-32. *Setting the toolbar's Justify-Content to space-between*

Figure 4-33. *Result of the toolbar's Justify-Content to space-between*

You can also center the label vertically and horizontally by setting the Align attributes (Figure 4-34).

Figure 4-34. *Centering the text in the title label*

Since you need to add a clicked event to the Build Settings ToolbarButton in C# code afterward, you must specify a name for it so you can use it to query for the button. Name the button control build-settings at the inspector panel (Figure 4-35).

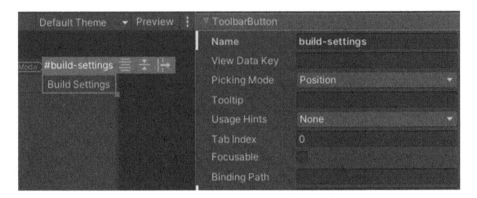

Figure 4-35. *Setting a custom name for the VisualElement*

Lastly, drag in a `ListView` control from the library panel to the same level as the toolbar in the hierarchy (Figure 4-36). Then set the `ListView`'s name to `scene-list` in the inspector panel.

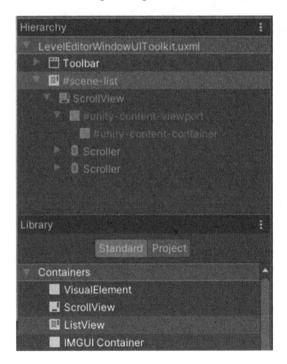

Figure 4-36. *The name will be displayed in the hierarchy in the UI Builder.*

So you now have the main layout of the level editor window. You are going to create a separate UXML layout for the list item representing each level! Close the current UI Builder window. To create a UXML file, in the project window, right-click and go to Create > UI Toolkit > UI Document. Upon creating the UI Document, name it LevelListItem. See Figure 4-37.

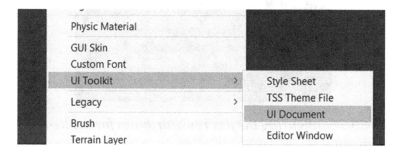

Figure 4-37. *Creating a new UI Document for the LevelListItem*

Get the UI Builder open by double-clicking the new UI Document and create the item hierarchy shown in Figure 4-38. I will go through the controls one by one.

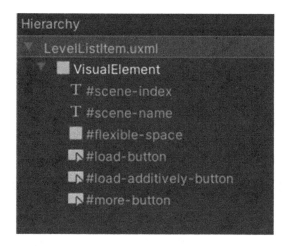

Figure 4-38. *Overall hierarchy of the item layout*

103

First, from the library panel, drag in a `VisualElement` as the container for the item. Set its Flex Direction to row (second-to-last option of the Flex Direction) in the inspector panel (Figure 4-39).

Figure 4-39. *Configuring the flex row attributes for the item VisualElement*

Next, drag in two Label controls as the children of the container and name them `scene-index` and `scene-name`. Drag in an empty `VisualElement` after the `scene-name` label and name it as `flexible-space` and set its Flex Grow value to 1 (Figure 4-40), so that it can fill in the empty space in between.

Figure 4-40. *Configuring the grow value for the flexible-space VisualElement*

Finally, drag in three Button controls after flexible-space and name them load-button, load-additively-button, and more-button. The names will be useful for finding the Buttons later on in the code. Set the Text property of the three buttons to Load, Load Additively, and ..., respectively.

After setting up the item layout, it should look something similar to Figure 4-41. Next, go back to the C# file and set up the GUI logic and behavior.

Figure 4-41. *Overall layout of the item*

Getting back to the editor code in the CreateGUI method, after cloning the layout with visualTree.CloneTree(root); you can use the Q method to query your target VisualElement with a specific name from the instantiated layout. First, you must set up your ListView by setting the makeItem function to a lambda, returning a new item layout by instantiating from the UXML and bindItem action to the lambda that binds the data to the template items. Finally, assign the scene data source to itemsSource, so the ListView will know how many items it needs to prepare (Listing 4-22).

Listing 4-22. Setting the ListView with Data Source and Loading the Item Layout from the UXML File

```
var sceneList = root.Q<ListView>("scene-list");
var itemTree = AssetDatabase.LoadAssetAtPath<VisualTreeAsset>
("Assets/Editor/LevelListItem.uxml");
sceneList.makeItem = () => itemTree.Instantiate();
sceneList.bindItem = (element, index) =>
```

```
{
    element.Q<Label>("scene-index").text = index.ToString();
};
sceneList.itemsSource = EditorBuildSettings.scenes;
```

Now if you compile and jump back to the editor window, you should
see a list of items, like Figure 4-42.

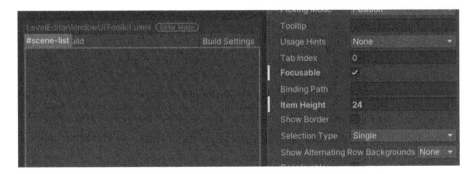

Figure 4-42. *The result of setting up the ListView*

To further adjust the height of each item in the ListView,
you can simply set it in the UI Builder by opening the
LevelEditorWindowUIToolkit.uxml file (Figure 4-43).

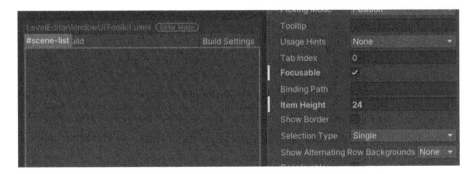

Figure 4-43. *Adjusting the ItemHeight attribute of the ListView in UI*
Builder

Now that you have the ListView hooking up the item view and data properly, let's start finalizing the bindItem callback to hook up the button-clicked event for each scene item (Listing 4-23).

Listing 4-23. Binding the Data Source to the Item's View in the bindItem Callback

```
sceneList.bindItem = (element, index) =>
{
    // Index Label
    element.Q<Label>("scene-index").text = index.ToString();
    // Scene Label
    var scene = EditorBuildSettings.scenes[index];
    var sceneName = Path.GetFileNameWithoutExtension(scene.
    path);
    element.Q<Label>("scene-name").text = sceneName;
    // Button Callbacks
    element.Q<Button>("load-button").clicked += () =>
    {
        if (EditorSceneManager.SaveCurrentModifiedScenes
        IfUserWantsTo())
            EditorSceneManager.OpenScene(scene.path);
    };
    element.Q<Button>("load-additive      -button").clicked +=
() =>
    {
        if (EditorSceneManager.SaveCurrentModifiedScenes
        IfUserWantsTo())
            EditorSceneManager.OpenScene(scene.path,
            OpenSceneMode.Additive);
    };
    element.Q<Button>("more-button").clicked += () =>
```

```
    {
        var menu = new GenericMenu();
        menu.AddItem(new GUIContent("Locate"), false, () =>
        {
            var sceneAsset = AssetDatabase.LoadAssetAtPath<Scene
            Asset>(scene.path);
            EditorGUIUtility.PingObject(sceneAsset);
        });
        menu.ShowAsContext();
    };
};
```

Lastly, after populating the items, remember to add a button-clicked callback for the build settings button to open the Build Setting window quicker. See Listing 4-24.

Listing 4-24. Adding a Clicked Callback to the Build Setting Button in the Toolbar

```
root.Q<Button>("build-settings").clicked += () =>
{
    EditorApplication.ExecuteMenuItem("File/Build Settings...");
};
```

Before wrapping up, you also need to make sure when the build settings scene is changed, you also update the ListView. You can do that by having a OnFocus method in your editor window, so whenever the window is focused by a user, the data source is updated once. See Listing 4-25.

Listing 4-25. Refreshing the Data Source of the ListView Each Time
the User Focus Is Back to the EditorWindow

```
private void OnFocus()
{
    ListView sceneList = rootVisualElement.Q<ListView>("scene-
    list");
    sceneList.itemsSource = EditorBuildSettings.scenes;
    sceneList.Refresh();
}
```

And now you have a working level editor window with UI Toolkit using
UI Builder (Figure 4-44) by opening the window via Window > Level Editor
UI Toolkit.

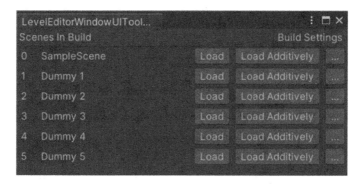

Figure 4-44. *Final result of the LevelEditor with UI Toolkit*

Summary

In this chapter, you used Unity's UI Toolkit for editor GUI authoring, which
uses VisualElement. You can create the UI once and let the underlying
layout system do the layout calculation without drawing each frame of the
GUI yourself, like you did with IMGUI.

With UI Toolkit, you can create a custom `editor`, `PropertyDrawer`, and `EditorWindow`, just like in IMGUI. However, for `PropertyDrawer`, you need to handle the parent custom editor specially to make sure it is also using UI Toolkit by implementing a custom editor for your component.

Congrats! You learned about creating `VisualElements` from code (`Button`, `PropertyField`, `FloatField`, etc.) or using the UI Builder for direct and visual GUI creation. You can then load the UXML `UIDocument` via the file path and instantiate the layout to display it. To reference a specific `VisualElement`, you can set a specific name for that element in the code or UXML file via UI Builder. Next, you use the Q method to query that specific name.

By understanding both UI Toolkit and IMGUI, you can decide which method will best suit your editor project and take a great advantage of your choice.

CHAPTER 5

Object Spawner Tool Using EditorTool and ScriptableObject

In this chapter, you are going to create a little object spawner editor tool to learn how editor scripting with IMGUI can be applied in a practical scenario and to explore some advanced editor topics such as EditorTool and ScriptableObject in this context.

Here are the key editor classes and terms used in the editor tool project:

- EditorTool (custom tools for scene view like move, rotate, scale)

- Handles (3D and 2D drawing and control in scene view)

- ScriptableObject (used for data storage and easy serialization in the editor)

- IMGUI (2D editor GUI drawing)

- ASMDEF (organizing your code into separate Assemblies)

© Benny Kok 2021
B. Kok, *Beginning Unity Editor Scripting*, https://doi.org/10.1007/978-1-4842-7167-4_5

Overview of the Tool

The idea of the tool is a prefab spawner system that allows a level designer to easily spawn a random group of prefabs right in the scene view by implementing a custom `EditorTool` for handling the scene view interaction and gizmos, and then use `ScriptableObject` to create a `Spawner` asset to store the prefab brush data like prefab reference, spawn count, and so on and a `ScriptableObject` that also contains the logic used to spawn the prefabs.

Figure 5-1 shows a glimpse of the final view of the custom tool: a circle gizmo shows up on your mouse hover in the scene view and allows you to paint on the ground when you click it. The Spawner preset can be selected in the bottom left overlay window in the scene view.

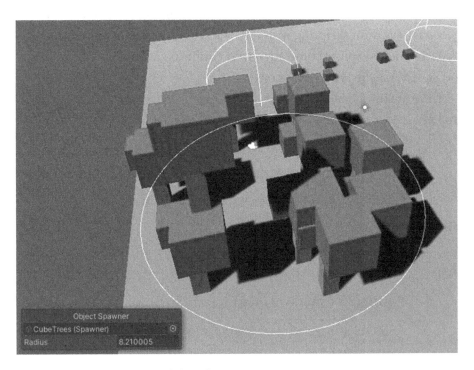

Figure 5-1. *Overview of the object spawner*

EditorTool

EditorTool is a class that you can implement and use to create a custom scene view-based tool like the move/rotate/scale tool that allows you directly manipulated the scene object with a corresponding GUI (Figure 5-2). Selecting each tool gives you different GUI handles, and each tool handles the scene view interaction differently, which provides a lot of flexibility. In conjunction with the Handles API, you can draw a custom GUI and control in the scene view with world space transform.

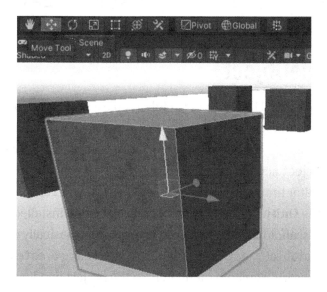

Figure 5-2. *Move tool selected*

For custom tools, you can access them in the dropdown of the last item in the toolbar tray (Figure 5-3).

113

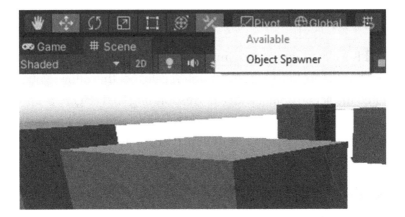

Figure 5-3. *Custom tools appear in the dropdown*

ScriptableObject

ScriptableObject in Unity is very useful. It's like a MonoBehaviour but it doesn't need to attach to any GameObject. Each instance can be saved and serialized as an asset file in the editor, and you can reference the ScriptableObject across scenes and other assets as well. It can also be run in both editor time and runtime. To easily create a ScriptableObject object, with the **Unity Code Snippet** VS code extension installed, it will automatically scaffold the class for you (Figure 5-4). It basically extends from the ScriptableObject class (Listing 5-1) and has a CreateAssetMenu attribute that inserts a custom menu item in the project window (Figure 5-5) for you to create an instance of your ScriptableObject as an asset file.

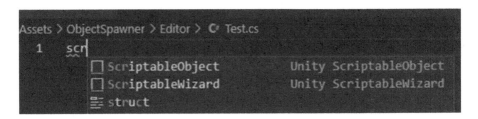

Figure 5-4. *Using the snippet to quickly create a ScriptableObject class*

114

Listing 5-1. A Simple ScriptableObject with a Float Field

```
using UnityEngine;

[CreateAssetMenu(fileName = "Test", menuName = "Beginning Unity
Editor Scripting/Test")]
public class Test : ScriptableObject {
    public float someFloat;
}
```

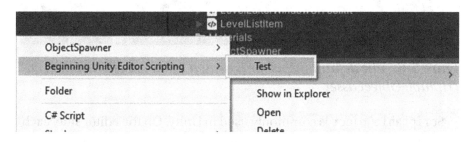

Figure 5-5. *CreateAssetMenuAttribute lets you create the asset file for the ScriptableObject via the menu*

By selecting the ScriptableObject asset file, you can edit the object fields directly in the inspector (Figure 5-6).

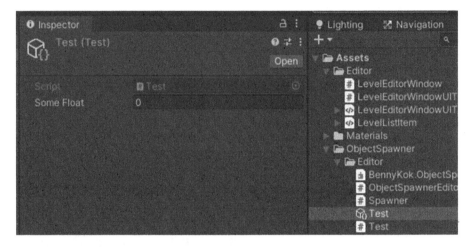

Figure 5-6. *The default inspector is drawn upon selection of the ScriptableObject asset*

ScriptableObject is commonly used in Unity. On the editor side, each EditorWindow and Editor class is also a ScriptableObject. Their state can get serialized easily and preserved by the Assembly reload when you edit the scripts. In another example, each clip in the timeline (Figure 5-7) is also a ScriptableObject under the hood, and the TimelineAsset itself is also a ScriptableObject. So, every change in the timeline can get serialized by the editor and is able to support the undo system easily.

Figure 5-7. *Timeline*

Setting Up the Project Structure

Let's begin by laying out the project structure of the tool. In this example, you will follow the Unity package's folder structure[1] with an asmdef setup. First, you create the parent folder with the asset name. Call it ObjectSpawner. Next, create two folders, Editor and Runtime, for the editor code and runtime code, respectively (Figure 5-8). Then set up the asmdef file for each script folder by right-clicking and locating the menu item named Create/Assembly Definition. Create one under the Editor folder and name it XXX.ObjectSpawner.Editor and one under the Runtime folder and name it XXX.ObjectSpawner.

Figure 5-8. *Creating the Editor and Runtime folders*

Next, make sure the Name property of both asmdefs matches the filename to keep everything consistent. The Name property is the actual name of this assembly, which can be different from the filename, but it's better to keep them the same to avoid confusion. You might also notice the Root Namespace property. By setting it, upon creating the C# script in that folder inside Unity, the namespace will be included in the C# file, which is convenient.

---

[1] https://docs.unity3d.com/Manual/cus-layout.html

Since you will be using the runtime code in your editor code, you need to reference the runtime asmdef to the editor asmdef by dragging it to the Assembly Definition Reference array in the editor asmdef (Figure 5-9).

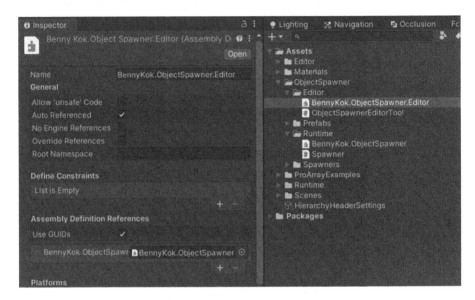

Figure 5-9. *Linking the runtime asmdef to the editor asmdef*

Next, in the editor asmdef, mark it as Editor only in the Platform section (Figure 5-10). You can simply deselect all and select the Editor checkbox. Next, remember to apply the setting and let it recompile.

Figure 5-10. *Marking as editor only for the editor asmdef*

Scriptable Structure

Before implementing the EditorTool, you first lay down the data structure
for storing the spawner's data. Create a ScriptableObject class by creating
a C# file named Spawner under the Runtime folder (Figure 5-11). Note that
if your ScriptableObject is only used in the editor, you can only put the
file in the Editor folder. However, in this case, your spawner can be also
used in runtime for other purposes, such as spawning in runtime.

Figure 5-11. *Creating the Spawner.cs file*

Next, extend your class with ScriptableObject, and you usually wrap the class in a namespace with the same name as the asmdef to keep it consistent. In the Spawner ScriptableObject, you store the target prefabs, count for spawning objects, and autoGround bool for whether to do a raycast to ground when the object is spawned to make sure it will be placed correctly on the ground. Lastly, the Spawner class also handles the actual spawning logic (Listing 5-2).

Listing 5-2. Spawner ScriptableObject

```
using UnityEngine;

namespace BennyKok.ObjectSpawner
{
    [CreateAssetMenu(fileName = "Spawner", menuName =
    "ObjectSpawner/Spawner")]
    public class Spawner : ScriptableObject
    {
        public int spawnCount = 10;
        public GameObject[] prefabs;

        [Header("Auto Ground")]
        public bool autoGround = true;
        public float raycastHeight = 10;
        public float groundOffset;

        public void SpawnObjects(Vector3 position, float
        radius)
        {
                // Spawn objects logic
        }
    }
}
```

Next, you are going to implement the SpawnObjects method, which will take in a world position and radius for spawning the group of prefabs. First, you create a parent GameObject to hold all of the spawned objects. Next, you use #if preprocessor UNITY_EDITOR to check and register a custom undo for the parent object you just created if you are in the editor. Note that the child GameObject will also be taken into account for the undo operation. Finally, you loop through your target object count and instantiate each random prefab in a random location in the radius around the target position. You also check if autoGround is enabled. You do a raycast and look for the proper ground position along the Y axis to make sure the object is not spawned under the ground.

For instantiating with a prefab connection in the editor time, you must use the PrefabUtility class, which will help instantiate a prefab while keeping its connection. If you use the Instantiate method only, it will break the prefab connection. Since PrefabUtility is an Editor class, you also wrap the #if preprocessor around the instantiation logic. See Listing 5-3.

Listing 5-3. SpawnObjects Method

```
public void SpawnObjects(Vector3 position, float radius)
{
    var stampParentObject = new GameObject("Stamp - " + name);
    stampParentObject.transform.position = position;

    #if UNITY_EDITOR
  UnityEditor.Undo.RegisterCreatedObjectUndo(stampParentObject,
  "Create " + stampParentObject.name);
    #endif

    for (int i = 0; i < spawnCount; i++)
    {
        var randomPrefabs = prefabs[Random.Range(0, prefabs.
        Length)];
```

```
var randomPosition2D = Random.insideUnitCircle *
radius;
var targetPositionX = position.x + randomPosition2D.x;
var targetPositionZ = position.z + randomPosition2D.y;
var targetPositionY = position.y;
var targetPosition = new Vector3(targetPositionX,
targetPositionY, targetPositionZ);
if (autoGround)
{
    var raycastOrigin = targetPosition;
    raycastOrigin.y += raycastHeight;
    if (Physics.Raycast(raycastOrigin, Vector3.down,
    out var result, raycastHeight))
        targetPosition.y = result.point.y +
        groundOffset;
}

 #if UNITY_EDITOR
var target = UnityEditor.PrefabUtility.
InstantiatePrefab(randomPrefab, stampParentObject.
transform) as GameObject;
target.transform.position = targetPosition;
#else
Instantiate(randomPrefab, targetPosition, Quaternion.
identity, stampParentObject.transform);
#endif
    }
}
```

Implementing a Custom EditorTool

Let's get started with the actual tool code by implementing a custom
EditorTool class first. Create a new C# script file and place it in the Editor
folder (Figure 5-12).

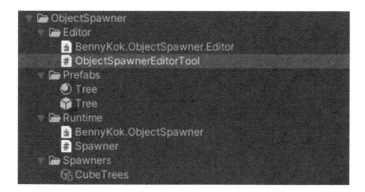

Figure 5-12. *Creating the ObjectSpawnerEditorTool.cs file*

Next, extend your class with the EditorTool class from the
UnityEditor.EditorTool namespace. In your custom EditorTool class,
override the toolIcon property to return a custom icon for the tool bar
display, and then override the OnToolGUI method to implement your tool
GUI logic later (Listing 5-4).

Listing 5-4. Custom EditorTool Implementation

```
using System;
using UnityEngine;
using UnityEditor;
using UnityEditor.EditorTools;

namespace BennyKok.ObjectSpawner.Editor
{
    [EditorTool("Object Spawner")]
```

```
public class ObjectSpawnerEditorTool : EditorTool
{
    [NonSerialized] private GUIContent toolIcon;
    public override GUIContent toolbarIcon
    {
        get
        {
            if (toolIcon == null) toolIcon =
            EditorGUIUtility.IconContent("GameObject On
            Icon", "Object Spawner");
            return toolIcon;
        }
    }
    public override void OnToolGUI(EditorWindow window)
    {
        // Tool GUI code
    }
}
}
```

After creating the custom tool class, if you jump back into Unity, you should see the option named Object Spawner when you click the last button to the right of the tool bar (Figure 5-13). By selecting the tool, your OnToolGUI method will call everything to let the selected tool handle its scene GUI.

Figure 5-13. *Accessing the Object Spawner EditorTool you just created*

Next, you need more fields to store the state of the tool (Listing 5-5). See Table 5-1 for each field's usage. Since the EditorTool is also a ScriptableObject, in this case, any serialized field will be preserved across the script's recompilation. For instance, if you change the tool's class, the serialized field's value will stay there even after Unity recompiles and reloads the Assembly of your code. Also, you can mark some fields as NonSerialized if you don't want them to be serialized.

Listing 5-5. Declaring Required Fields

```
[NonSerialized] private Rect toolWindowRect = new Rect(10, 0,
260f, 0f);
private Spawner selectedSpawner;
private float spawnRadius = 2;
[NonSerialized] private bool mouseDown;
[NonSerialized] private Vector2 mouseDownPosition;
```

Table 5-1. *Fields and Usage*

Field	Usage
toolWindowRect	The rect for the overlay window in the scene view
selectedSpawner	The selected spawner reference
spawnRadius	The radius to spawn
mouseDown	If the mouse was down previously
mouseDownPosition	The down position for the mouse position

After declaring the required fields, let's implement a little overlay window (Listing 5-6) that will be anchored at the lower left corner of the scene view, which lets you draw some extra GUI and act as a mini inspector for the user to change the spawn radius and set the prefab spawner (Figure 5-14). By using the GUILayout.Window method, it takes in id and rect (position and size) methods for GUI drawing and the window name.

Listing 5-6. Drawing an Overlay Window in the Scene View

```
public void DrawToolWindow(int id)
{
    selectedSpawner = EditorGUILayout.
    ObjectField(selectedSpawner, typeof(Spawner), false) as
    Spawner;
    spawnRadius = EditorGUILayout.FloatField("Radius",
    spawnRadius);
}

public override void OnToolGUI(EditorWindow window)
{
    toolWindowRect.y = window.position.height - toolWindowRect.
    height - 10;
    toolWindowRect = GUILayout.Window(45, toolWindowRect,
    DrawToolWindow, "Object Spawner");

    // Event logic
}
```

Figure 5-14. *Result of the overlay window*

Next, to handle the hover interaction in the OnToolGUI method (Listing 5-7), you first get the current mouse position and use it to create a ray pointing to the world, which will use the raycast to check if the mouse is hovering above the ground or any collider.

You also want the user to be able to drag to resize the spawn radius and then release the mouse to trigger the spawn. For the level design process to be more intuitive, you need to cache the mouseDownPosition and use it instead of the current mouse position for raycasting when user has pressed down the first time and resized the radius.

Finally, when you check if the mouse is correctly hovering on any collider, then using the Handles class you can draw out a circle wire to indicate the spawn radius in the scene view.

Listing 5-7. Raycasting from Mouse Position and Drawing a Wire Disc

```
var ray = HandleUtility.GUIPointToWorldRay(mouseDown ?
mouseDownPosition : Event.current.mousePosition);
bool hitGround = Physics.Raycast(ray, out var result, 100);
if (hitGround)
{
    Handles.DrawWireDisc(result.point, Vector3.up,
    spawnRadius);
}
```

After raycasting and drawing the handles, in the OnToolGUI method, to properly handle the user interaction, you first get a control ID for the current operation with EditorGUIUtility.GetControlID to later set to the GUIUtility.hotControl to prevent the mouse event triggering the scene view box selection when dragging. Next, use a switch for the current event type via Event.current and handle each event individually (Listing 5-8). See Table 5-2 for a detailed explanation on how to handle the interaction in different events in this scenario.

Listing 5-8. Event Handling

```
var controlId = EditorGUIUtility.GetControlID(FocusType.
Passive);
switch (Event.current.type)
{
    case EventType.MouseDown:
        if (Event.current.button == 0 && Event.current.
        modifiers == EventModifiers.None)
        {
            GUIUtility.hotControl = controlId;
            mouseDown = true;
            mouseDownPosition = Event.current.mousePosition;
            Event.current.Use();
        }
        break;
    case EventType.MouseDrag:
        if (mouseDown)
        {
            spawnRadius += EditorGUIUtility.
            PixelsToPoints(Event.current.delta).x / 100;
            window.Repaint();
        }
        break;
    case EventType.MouseMove:
        window.Repaint();
        break;
    case EventType.MouseLeaveWindow:
    case EventType.MouseUp:
        if (mouseDown && hitGround && selectedSpawner)
        {
```

```
        selectedSpawner.SpawnObjects(result.point,
        spawnRadius);
    }
    mouseDown = false;
    break;
}
```

Table 5-2. *Events and Explanation*

Event	Explanation
EventType.MouseDown	If the mouse down event with left mouse button and no other keyboard modifiers is on, you cache the current mouse position and consume the event with Event.current.Use(). By setting the hot control, you can avoid the interaction being used for other actions (e.g. box selection when dragging in the scene view).
EventType.MouseDrag	When the mouse begins dragging, you add the mouse delta movement to the radius. Also, by using EditorGUIUtility.PixelsToPoints you can make sure the delta value is persistent across different DPI monitor displays.
EventType.MouseMove	Repainting the scene view to update the wire disc circle handles.
EventType.MouseLeaveWindow and EventType.MouseUp	When the drag is outside the current windows and the mouse is up, EventType.MouseLeaveWindow will be the current event. If the user mouse is up while the mouse is still in current window, you have the EventType.MouseUp event. For both events, you perform the spawn action which calls to the selectedSpawner.SpawnObjects().

Finally, you will be able to see the wired disc (Figure 5-15) and drag to resize the spawn radius (Figure 5-16).

Figure 5-15. *Wire disc on mouse hover location*

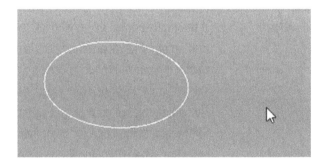

Figure 5-16. *Dragging to increase the spawn radius*

Wrapping Up

With the custom `EditorTool` implemented property, now you can set up some `Spawner ScriptableObjects` for the tool to spawn (Figure 5-17).

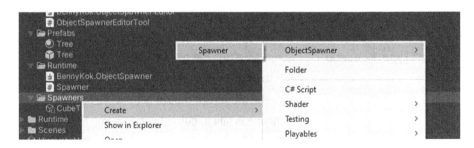

Figure 5-17. *Creating a Spawner asset*

Next, you can create a dummy tree model in Unity (Figure 5-18).

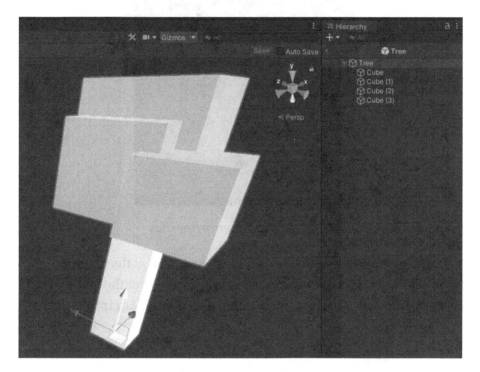

Figure 5-18. *Creating a dummy tree prefab with some cubes*

Or you can use your custom prefabs and assign them to the Spawner for random spawning (Figure 5-19).

Figure 5-19. *Configuring the Spawner properties*

If you now switch over to the Object Spawner tool in the tool bar
(Figure 5-20), you will see your little overlay window over the bottom left
corner (Figure 5-21) where you can assign the Spawner ScriptableObject.

Figure 5-20. *Switching to Object Spawner in the toolbar*

Figure 5-21. *Selecting the tree spawner in the overlay window*

Now you can start spawning some prefabs in the scene randomly. Hold and drag to resize the spawn radius. Releasing will trigger the spawn (Figure 5-22) since you also implemented the undo. You can undo the spawn just like any native Unity tool.

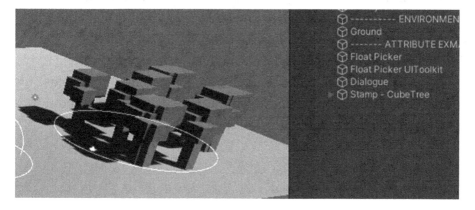

Figure 5-22. *Spawning a set of prefabs in the scene*

Summary

In this chapter, you went through a tool project example by utilizing editor scripting with IMGUI and other things learned in previous chapters. You also learned some interesting editor topics such as EditorTool and ScriptableObject. EditorTool lets you extend the scene view functionalities and handle custom scene view interaction, and ScriptableObject acts as a data store that lets you easily serialize a custom object as an asset file in the project.

With this project example, you learned how to structure a plugin project with asmdef, using the Handles class to draw a 3D GUI in the scene view and handling event interaction in the custom EditorTool.

You should now have a bigger picture of how each aspect of the editor can be chained together to create some interesting helper editor tools or help with specific or unique use cases. For example, this Object Spawner can be further expanded into supporting more parameters and spawns with more variation, or even take a specific predefined pattern to spawn a natural biome or a village configuration, which could save level designers tons of time and unlock new possibilities.

There is much more to explore with the Editor API. There are many more APIs like `EditorTool` that let you build upon existing functionalities in Unity, and many are one Google search away for their official documentation or forum thread. I encourage you to explore more!

In the next chapters, I will cover the case studies for my assets plus custom editor implementations, which will give you more clues and insights about editor scripting in published assets.

CHAPTER 6

Case Study: ProArray

In this chapter, I will take you through my asset **ProArray** (Figure 6-1) from the original idea to implementation and from prerelease preparation to post-release analysis. Lastly, I will share the lessons I learned over the course of the project.

The purpose of this chapter is to give you a glimpse into how editor scripting is applied to published assets and to share some publishing insight with you. I will also share and explain some extra editor examples used in ProArray.

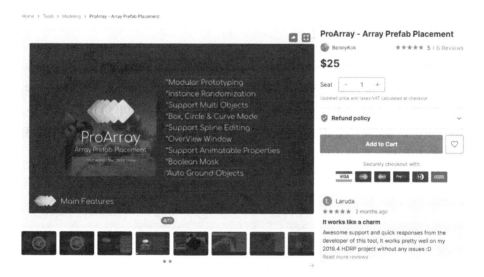

Figure 6-1. *ProArray's Asset Store page*

B. Kok, *Beginning Unity Editor Scripting*, https://doi.org/10.1007/978-1-4842-7167-4_6

Idea and Concept

ProArray is an array prefab placement tool. It all started back in 2017 when I had to do a lot of manual repetitive object placement work during level design in my Unity projects. For instance, I wanted to randomly scatter some prefabs on the ground, but doing it manually was time consuming and didn't seem viable. At that time, I was also playing around with 3D modeling software, such as Blender. I became aware of the Array Modifier concept found in most 3D modeling software, which gives you a lot of flexibility with repeating structures. Eventually, my solution was to create an array modifier-like component in Unity for handling prefab placement in a manageable way. With ProArray, you can configure the prefabs to spawn in a box mode, along a circle, or even follow a curve. You can even apply random properties on the prefabs for more level design variation.

Implementation

I started working on this idea immediately. The initial implementation was pretty simple. At the core is a `MonoBehaviour` class that stores all of the parameters and has a custom editor to handle instantiation of the prefabs. Implementing the custom editor (Figure 6-2) for the component allows me to have more control over the workflow of using the tool.

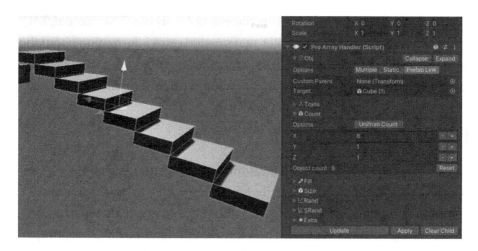

Figure 6-2. *ProArray's editor with a vertical layout*

Structure

The tool's scripts are separated into two major folders (Figure 6-3): Editor (for editor-specific scripts) and Runtime (for runtime-specific scripts) with an asmdef setup, which I talked about in the previous chapter. I tried to keep the naming of the scripts folders the same as the UPM package structure to make it easier to communicate with users since the folder structure will be familiar to them. I will talk in depth about UPM packages in the later part of the book.

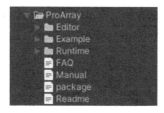

Figure 6-3. *Folder structure of the ProArray asset*

The `Example` folder is for storing the examples scenes. The manual, FAQ, and Readme files are plain text files that provide extra information about the asset. You can also include a PDF for a quick start guide about your asset as it can be more visual since you can insert screenshots into the PDF.

Editor Foldout Layout

One challenging aspect during development was getting the editor UX right. More and more properties have been added to the ProArray component and it's hard to navigate. I didn't want to confuse the user with any grouping of the properties. Therefore, to differentiate different groups of properties, I went with a vertical foldout grouping layout at first.

Listing 6-1 shows a simplified example of the vertical layout with icons in each of the foldouts (Figure 6-4). You can either follow along or check out the source repo for this book and play with it directly.

By using `EditorGUIUtility.IconContent` I can load in any built-in icons from the editor. You can reference them by the name of the icon. The list of built-in icons can be easily found online[1]. With `IconContent,` the icon texture is packed into a `GUIContent` and you can use it with most IMGUI methods that take in `GUIContent`.

By using the `EditorGUILayout.BeginFoldoutHeaderGroup` method, you can draw out the foldout layout and only draw the children's content if the method returns true, meaning the foldout is opened. You also need to cache the returned result to an bool array to keep the state of the editor.

---

[1]https://github.com/halak/unity-editor-icons

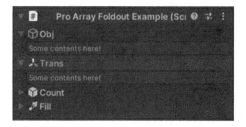

Figure 6-4. *Foldout with icons*

Listing 6-1. Custom Editor Foldout with Icons

```
using UnityEngine;
#if UNITY_EDITOR
using UnityEditor;
#endif
public class ProArrayFoldoutExample : MonoBehaviour { }

#if UNITY_EDITOR
[UnityEditor.CustomEditor(typeof(ProArrayFoldoutExample))]
public class ProArrayFoldoutExampleEditor : UnityEditor.Editor
{
    public GUIContent[] tabs1;
    private bool[] foldouts = new bool[4];
    private void OnEnable()
    {
        tabs1 = new[]
        {
            IconContent("GameObject Icon", "Obj"),
            IconContent("Transform Icon", "Trans"),
            IconContent("Prefab Icon", "Count"),
            IconContent("eyeDropper.Large", "Fill")
        };
    }
```

```
public GUIContent IconContent(string name, string label)
{
    GUIContent guiContent = EditorGUIUtility.
    IconContent(name);
    guiContent.text = label;
    return guiContent;
}

public override void OnInspectorGUI()
{
    for (int i = 0; i < tabs1.Length; i++)
    {
        foldouts[i] = EditorGUILayout.BeginFoldoutHeader
        Group(foldouts[i], tabs1[i]);
        if (foldouts[i])
            EditorGUILayout.HelpBox("Some contents here!",
            MessageType.None);
        EditorGUILayout.EndFoldoutHeaderGroup();
    }
}
}
#endif
```

Custom Toolbar Layout

The vertical foldout layout is good, but when everything is expanded, it takes up a lot of space in the inspector. I went with a toolbar layout as the default editor layout eventually (Figure 6-5). With the toolbar layout, the user can switch between different sections by clicking the icon in the toolbar and only one section will be shown at a time.

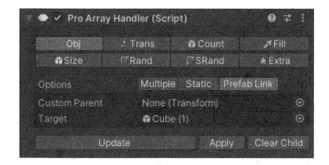

Figure 6-5. *ProArray's toolbar layout editor*

Listing 6-2 shows a custom editor example to implement a toolbar layout with the GUILayout.Toolbar method. This example shares a similar code structure with the vertical foldout grouping layout above. You still need the array of IconContents for loading the built-in icons, and you have an integer field for storing the selected tab. In the OnInspectorGUI method, by calling GUILayout.Toolbar, it will draw the toolbar layout and return the current selected tab. The example result is shown in Figure 6-6.

Listing 6-2. Custom Editor Toolbar Layout with Icons

```
using UnityEngine;

#if UNITY_EDITOR
using UnityEditor;
#endif

public class ProArrayEditorExample : MonoBehaviour { }

#if UNITY_EDITOR
[UnityEditor.CustomEditor(typeof(ProArrayEditorExample))]
public class ProArrayEditorExampleEditor : UnityEditor.Editor
{
    public GUIContent[] tabs1;
    private int selectedTab;
```

```
    private void OnEnable()
    {
        tabs1 = new[]
        {
            IconContent("GameObject Icon", "Obj"),
            IconContent("Transform Icon", "Trans"),
            IconContent("Prefab Icon", "Count"),
            IconContent("eyeDropper.Large", "Fill")
        };
    }

    public GUIContent IconContent(string name, string label)
    {
        GUIContent guiContent = EditorGUIUtility.
        IconContent(name);
        guiContent.text = label;
        return guiContent;
    }

    public override void OnInspectorGUI()
    {
        var iconSize = new Vector2(12, 12);
        var originalIconSize = EditorGUIUtility.GetIconSize();
        using (new EditorGUILayout.HorizontalScope())
        {
            EditorGUIUtility.SetIconSize(iconSize);
            selectedTab = GUILayout.Toolbar(selectedTab, tabs1);
            EditorGUIUtility.SetIconSize(originalIconSize);
        }
    }
}
#endif
```

Figure 6-6. *Example toolbar layout editor with icons*

Custom Animatable Properties Support

ProArray has a unique aspect that some properties can be animated in runtime without a huge performance cost of recreating all the prefabs. For instance, the random properties (Figure 6-7) can be animated with Unity's Animation System.

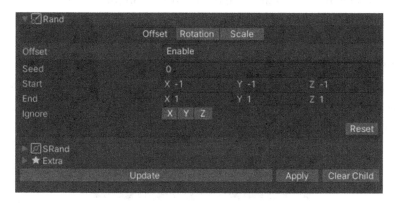

Figure 6-7. *The Random section of the ProArray editor*

Using Unity's Animation System with custom properties, there is a way to get notified when the animation values are being applied[2]: you have a method named OnDidApplyAnimationProperties (Listing 6-3) in your MonoBehaviour and then you can simply recalculate and update all the array prefabs' transforms accordingly in real time.

---

[2]https://forum.unity.com/threads/help-please-with-animation-component-
public-properties-custom-inspector.229328/

Listing 6-3. MonoBehaviour Callback After Animation Properties Are Applied

```
private void OnDidApplyAnimationProperties()
{
    if (enabled)
        UpdateArrayObjectProperty();
}
```

Component Icon

You might have noticed that there is a custom icon for the ProArrayHandler component (Figure 6-8). It is actually very easy to configure a custom icon for your scripts and you can make your component easier to notice.

You need to prepare your icon first and import it as a texture in the project. Then, in your script's inspector, click the icon and pick your custom replacement (Figure 6-9).

Figure 6-8. *Custom component icon in the inspector*

Figure 6-9. *Select custom icons*

Once you pick a custom icon, you make some changes in the meta file of your script file (Figure 6-10), and that's how Unity remembers your custom icon for your script. This is a good example of the importance of the meta file in Unity.

```
 7  6    defaultReferences:
 8  7      - Target: {instanceID: 0}
 9  8      - TargetTransform: {instanceID: 0}
10  9      - CurveRoot: {instanceID: 0}
11 10    executionOrder: 0
12       icon: {fileID: 2800000, guid: a1d85c1c9e30c004cad3790915c8702a, type: 3}
   11    icon: {fileID: 5721338939258241955, guid: 0000000000000000d000000000000000, type: 0}
13 12    userData:
14 13    assetBundleName:
15 14    assetBundleVariant:
```

Figure 6-10. *Meta file changes with a custom icon (Fork – Git client)*

Scene Gizmos Icon

Next, the Gizmos icon is common for most built-in components in Unity. ProArray also has a Gizmos icon in the scene view (Figure 6-11). The Gizmos icon is the same component icon if you have it configured for your script file. For it to appear in the scene view, you must implement an OnDrawGizmos method in your component (Listing 6-4), even if you are not using it.

Figure 6-11. *Scene Gizmos icon example in ProArray*

Listing 6-4. Empty OnDrawGizmos method to enable the Gizmos Icon

```
public class ProArrayGizmosExmaple : MonoBehaviour
{
    private void OnDrawGizmos() { }
}
```

You can also change your component icon in the Gizmos dropdown in the scene view toolbar (Figure 6-12). Open the Gizmos dropdown and locate your component item. Pressing the icon dropdown next to your component name lets you pick the custom icon.

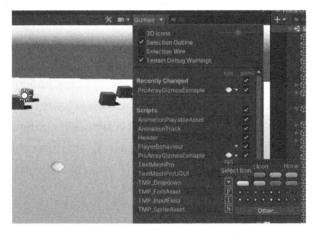

Figure 6-12. *Gizmos dropdown for changing the component icon*

Hierarchy Overlay

ProArray has an optional hierarchy button icon overlay (Figure 6-13) for the ProArrayHandler in the hierarchy, and it will show a popup menu for some quick action without going into the editor.

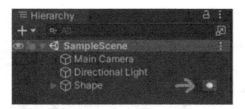

Figure 6-13. *Hierarchy overlay in ProArray*

Listing 6-5 shows an example of creating a hierarchy overlay by hooking a callback to the EditorApplication.hierarchyWindowItemOnGUI delegate in a custom class with an [InitializeOnLoad] attribute. By having this attribute, the static constructor of your class will be called when Unity loads your editor script.

Next, in the callback DrawHierarchyOverlay, you were given the instanceId and itemRect. You can then use the method EditorUtility. InstanceIDToObject to get the actual GameObject of the hierarchy item from the instanceId and check if the GameObject has the ProArray component. If the component exists, you draw out the overlay GUI with GUI.Button by passing in the rect for the position and size, and the icon texture as well.

To load the icon for your custom overlay, the easier way is to load the texture asset via the relative project path, but this will break if the asset is installed in a different location. One trick to reduce your scripts' dependencies on external icon resources is to first convert your icon to the base64 string format and then include the icon string directly in the code (Figure 6-14). Then you convert it back to a Texture2D on the first load. This will also prevent the editor icon from spamming in the user's assets browser. Your scripts can be self-contained and able to display the icon even if your asset is installed in another location, such as a UPM package.

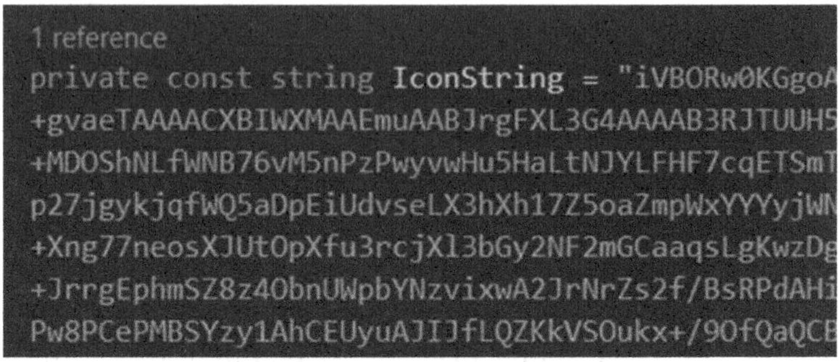

1 reference

private const string IconString = "iVBORwOKGgoA
+gvaeTAAAACXBIWXMAAEmuAABJrgFXL3G4AAAAB3RJTUUH5
+MDOShNLfWNB76vM5nPzPwyvwHu5HaLtNJYLFHF7cqETSmT
p27jgykjqfWQ5aDpEiUdvseLX3hXh17Z5oaZmpWxYYYyjWN
+Xng77neosXJUtOpXfu3rcjXl3bGy2NF2mGCaaqsLgKwzDg
+JrrgEphmSZ8z4ObnUWpbYNzvixwA2JrNrZs2f/BsRPdAHi
Pw8PCePMBSYzy1AhCEUyuAJIJfLQZKkVSOukx+/9OfQaQCE

Figure 6-14. *Icon string in base64 format*

Listing 6-5. Hierarchy Overlay Example

```
using System;
using UnityEditor;
using UnityEngine;

[InitializeOnLoad]
public class ProArrayHierarchyOverlay
{
    // Your icon converted to base64 string format
    private const string IconString = "...";
    private static Texture2D _hierarchyIconTexture;
    private static Texture2D HierarchyIconTexture
    {
        get
        {
            if (_hierarchyIconTexture == null)
            {
                _hierarchyIconTexture = new Texture2D(0, 0);
                _hierarchyIconTexture.LoadImage(Convert.
                FromBase64String(IconString));
            }
```

```
        return _hierarchyIconTexture;
    }
}

static ProArrayHierarchyOverlay()
{
    // Prevent overlapped callback
    EditorApplication.hierarchyWindowItemOnGUI -=
    DrawHierarchyOverlay;
    EditorApplication.hierarchyWindowItemOnGUI +=
    DrawHierarchyOverlay;
}

private static void DrawHierarchyOverlay(int instanceId,
Rect item    Rect)
{
    var r = new Rect(item    Rect);
    r.x = r.x + r.width - 20;
    r.width = 20;

    var currentGameObject = EditorUtility.
    InstanceIDToObject(instanceId) as GameObject;
    if (!currentGameObject) return;

    var toggleBoxComponent = currentGameObject.GetComponent
    <ProArrayToggleBoxExample>();
    if (!toggleBoxComponent) return;

    var originalIconSize = EditorGUIUtility.GetIconSize();

    var iconSize = new Vector2(12, 12);
    EditorGUIUtility.SetIconSize(iconSize);
```

```
    if (GUI.Button(r, HierarchyIconTexture))
    {
        var m = new GenericMenu();
        m.AddItem(new GUIContent("This is the menu"),
        false, () => { });
        m.ShowAsContext();
    }

    EditorGUIUtility.SetIconSize(originalIconSize);
  }
}
```

Toggle Box

In most `ProArray` components, you will see a horizontal list of toggles
(Figures 6-15 and 6-16), which makes the GUI more intuitive to use by
grouping the options in a single line.

Figure 6-15. *Toggle box for Offset, Rotation, and Scale*

Figure 6-16. *Toggle box for X, Y, and Z*

Listing 6-6 shows how to create the toggle list (Figure 6-17), which
could save a lot of space for your custom inspector. In the code, there
is a simple component with three boolean fields: x,y,x. Next, in the
custom editor, inside a horizontal scope, you draw the label by using the
`EditorGUILayout.PrefixLabel` and then you draw the three buttons

respectively using the custom `ToggleBox` method and pass in the `EditorStyles.miniButton` styles. In the `ToggleBox` method, you draw the actual toggle with the method `GUILayout.Toggle`.

Listing 6-6. Toggle Box Examples

```
using UnityEngine;

#if UNITY_EDITOR
using UnityEditor;
#endif

public class ProArrayToggleBoxExample : MonoBehaviour
{
    public bool x, y, z;
}

#if UNITY_EDITOR
[UnityEditor.CustomEditor(typeof(ProArrayToggleBoxExample))]
public class ProArrayToggleBoxExampleEditor : UnityEditor.
Editor
{
    SerializedProperty x, y, z;

    private void OnEnable()
    {
        x = serializedObject.FindProperty("x");
        y = serializedObject.FindProperty("y");
        z = serializedObject.FindProperty("z");
    }

    public override void OnInspectorGUI()
    {
        serializedObject.Update();
```

```
        using (new EditorGUILayout.HorizontalScope())
        {
            EditorGUILayout.PrefixLabel("Position");
            ToggleBox(x, "X", EditorStyles.miniButtonLeft);
            ToggleBox(y, "Y", EditorStyles.miniButtonMid);
            ToggleBox(z, "Z", EditorStyles.miniButtonRight);
        }
        serializedObject.ApplyModifiedProperties();
    }

    public void ToggleBox(SerializedProperty property, string
    label, GUIStyle style, float width = 20)
    {
        using (var scope = new EditorGUI.ChangeCheckScope())
        {
            var tempToggleValue = GUILayout.Toggle(property.
            boolValue, label, style, GUILayout.Width(width));

            // Only update the property value when the GUI is
            changed
            if (scope.changed)
                property.boolValue = tempToggleValue;
        }
    }
}
#endif
```

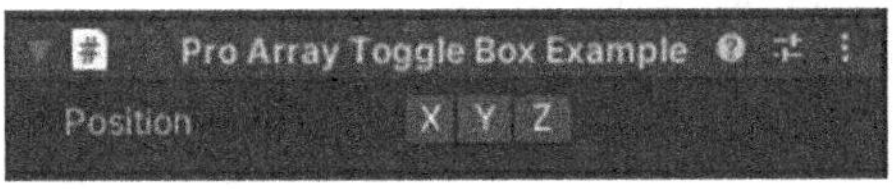

Figure 6-17. *Toggle box examples*

Prerelease Preparation

Once ProArray was near its final stage for release, I had to prepare the manual, demo scenes, screenshots, and description for the Asset Store.

For the manual, I included a simple .txt file with instructions on how to use ProArray (Figure 6-18). It could also be a .pdf containing a step-by-step guide or a link to the online documentation. In the later part of the book, I will explain in more detail how to create online manuals and documentation.

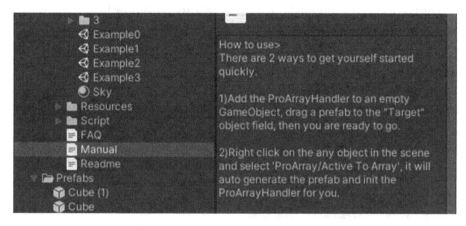

Figure 6-18. *The instructions for ProArray*

You must include an example scene (Figure 6-19) if you are publishing on the Asset Store, so users can see how the asset is intended to be used in different contexts. You don't have to be fancy with the demo. You just need to be able to showcase the important features, and a good demo scene will save you from getting general support queries about how to get started with using the asset.

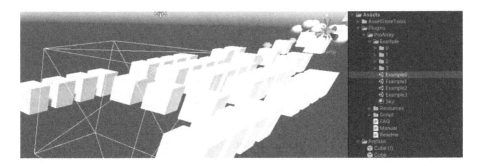

Figure 6-19. *Example scene in ProArray*

For the icon and screenshots, I used **Affinity Designer** for vector graphic editing (Figure 6-20). It comes with a straightforward interface and is packed with features. There are other alternatives, such as **Inkscape, GIMP,** and **Krita.**

Figure 6-20. *Editing screenshots, icons, and covers in Affinity Designer*

Post-Release Analysis

It's time to talk about the stats for **ProArray**. It was released in 2017, and the monthly net revenue has ranged from $20 to $80 USD (Figure 6-21, Table 6-1). Net revenue refers to the profit after the Asset Store's 30% cut.

From 2018 to 2019, I released two free assets on the store and that drove more traffic and boosted the visibility of ProArray.

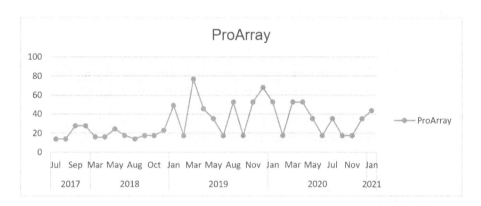

Figure 6-21. *Net revenue trend of ProArray from July 2017 to January 2021*

Table 6-1. *Net Revenue Table of ProArray from July 2017 to January 2021*

Sum of Net	Product	
Date	ProArray	Grand Total
2017	83.65	83.65
2018	145.24	145.24
2019	431.89	431.89
2020	332.49	332.49
2021	43.75	43.75
Grand Total	1037.02	1037.02

I'm being fully transparent by showing the revenue graph of ProArray throughout the years. You might not be impressed by the amount yet, but the point I am trying to make is everybody has to start somewhere. However, the goal is never only about selling tools; it is also about the tool itself and how it can empower others and yourself in the creative space of game development. Throughout the years, different people have told me how ProArray has helped them and how they use the tools in unexpected ways. It really keeps me motivated.

So if you are starting out, don't give up too soon if you are not seeing any immediate result. Sales is not the only indicator of gain; there is also invaluable experience and getting people to know about you. Don't mistakenly think that selling game tools can make you rich on day one. You will lose track of your motivation for creating the tool. Instead, be passionate. Enjoy the hustle. The rest will come.

Summary

ProArray is my first asset release. I learned numerous things throughout the journey, such as how to create custom editors in Unity, how to package the asset, and how to prepare screenshots and the cover for the Asset Store. Not only did I gain experience and passive income by creating such a tool; it also paved the way to my best selling asset, **Rhythm Game Starter**, which I will be covering in the next chapter.

As a whole, ProArray is exactly what I set out to do at the beginning: solve the frustration of repetitive prefab placement during level design by utilizing editor scripting. It has been an enjoyable experience and journey.

CHAPTER 7

Case Study: Rhythm Game Starter

In this chapter, I will discuss my other asset, **Rhythm Game Starter** (Figure 7-1), from the original idea to implementation and from prerelease preparation to post-release analysis. Interestingly, this is my best-selling asset, compared to ProArray. The overall time taken for the first release was pretty short, and I will talk more about it in the following sections.

There will also be some custom editor examples in this chapter, but I won't get too specific into some of the complex editor parts of Rhythm Game Starter.

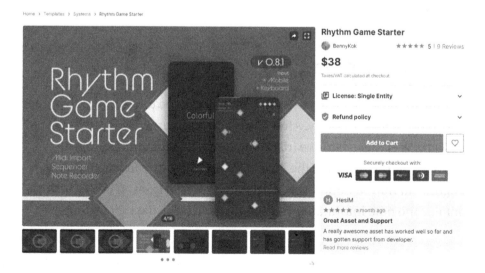

Figure 7-1. *Rhythm Game Starter's Asset Store page*

B. Kok, *Beginning Unity Editor Scripting*, https://doi.org/10.1007/978-1-4842-7167-4_7

Idea and Concept

Rhythm Game Starter is a game template asset specifically made for mobile rhythm games. The core feature is that the music notes in the game are synced with the playing music at the same bpm (beats per minute). Rhythm games are a tough problem to tackle. Most of the time, creators who want to create rhythm games have various questions like how to synchronize the music with the note movement, how to create and edit the note sequences, and how to handle the mobile input properly. These are also the questions that I researched before I got into the development of the asset.

The idea of creating a rhythm game emerged because one of my designer friends suggested making a rhythm game together. Since I have a music production background, I already had a clue as to how to utilize the MIDI (Musical Instrument Digital Interface) data exported from a DAW (digital audio workstation) into Unity for the sequence data. In the following sections, I will cover the editor implementation from part of the asset to give you a clue to what degree custom editor scripting is possible in Unity.

Implementation

After the initial idea, I had to create a little prototype to see how a rhythm game is possible with Unity. After doing some research, I knew that I could use AudioSettings.dspTime (digital signal processor time) for music synchronization instead of the Time.time in Unity. The first goal was to figure out how to import the MIDI data exported from a DAW, which contains the note information, so I could have some data for testing.

Editor Midi Import

For importing MIDI data, I needed to do some editor scripting. I used an open source .NET library named DryWetMIDI[1] to read the MIDI file (kudos to the author). Then I directly included the DLL file in the project and used its class in the editor code. By marking the DLL file as Editor only, I could exclude it from the final build since it was only used in the editor (Figure 7-2).

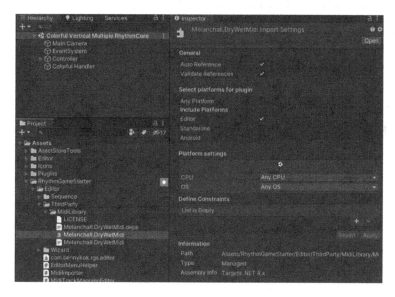

Figure 7-2. *Using a precompiled DLL library in Unity*

With the MIDI import figured out with the open source library, it was time to think about how note data could be stored in the project. You know it: ScriptableObject! Then I created a ScriptableObject called SongItem to store the imported note data, the audio clip reference, and also the target audio bpm.

---

[1]https://github.com/melanchall/drywetmidi

As mentioned in previous chapters, a custom ScriptableObject can be used to serialize data as an asset file easily, and now I could create a custom editor for it, the same as creating a custom editor for MonoBehaviour. A custom editor for ScriptableObject can be created by extending the Editor class and using the CustomEditor attribute to let Unity know that this custom editor is targeted for your own ScriptableObject class (Listing 7-1).

Listing 7-1. Custom Editor for ScriptableObject

```
using UnityEditor;

namespace RhythmGameStarter
{
    [CustomEditor(typeof(SongItem))]
    public class SongItemEditor : Editor
    {
        public override void OnInspectorGUI()
        {
            // Custom GUI for ScriptableObject
        }
    }
}
```

Now that I knew I could create a custom editor for ScriptableObject, I made a custom editor for the SongItem ScriptableObject, allowing users to pick the MIDI file to import right in the editor (Figure 7-3). In the editor code, I used the method provided by DryWetMIDI to import the MIDI file and I stored the data in the ScriptableObject.

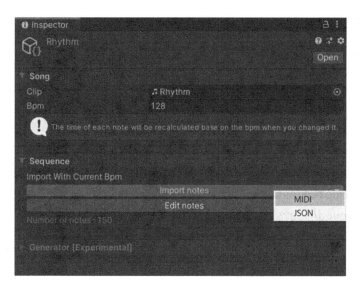

Figure 7-3. Importing file options in the custom ScriptableObject editor

AssetPostprocessor

In Rhythm Game Starter, to automate the import process for the MIDI file, I implemented a custom AssetPostprocessor, which could receive various callbacks related to asset import in the editor. Therefore, I could automatically create a SongItem ScriptableObject to store the incoming MIDI file imported by the user.

Listing 7-2 shows a brief example of creating a custom AssetPostprocessor by simply implementing a static method named OnPostprocessAllAssets. You are notified when any file is being imported and then you can filter out the file extension to look for the targeted MIDI file. In my case, I read in the imported MIDI file with DryWetMIDI and then created a SongItem ScriptableObject for it.

Listing 7-2. Using AssetPostprocessor

```
using UnityEditor;

namespace RhythmGameStarter
{
    public class MidiImporter : AssetPostprocessor
    {
        public static void OnPostprocessAllAssets(string[]
        importedAssets, string[] deletedAssets, string[]
        movedAssets, string[] movedFromAssetPaths)
        {
            foreach (string asset in importedAssets)
            {
                if (asset.EndsWith(".mid"))
                {
                    // Create a SongItem and import the midi data
                }
            }
        }
    }
}
```

"Abusing" PropertyDrawer in Rhythm Game Starter

I needed to create multiple component scripts to handle the actual rhythm game runtime logic, for instance StatsSystem for handling the combo, score, and missed logic in the rhythm game and TrackManager for handling the runtime note transform and synchronization. If I had to create a custom editor for each of the components, it would take a lot of time and it would be hard to manage as more and more components were added. What I did instead is I created an extensive set of custom attributes with `PropertyDrawer` and `DecoratorDrawer` so I could implement a custom GUI modularly. Then I reused the same GUI very easily just by declaring the attribute for each class field in the component.

For instance, Listing 7-3 is partial code of the `SongManager` component in Rhythm Game Starter to demonstrate the use of custom attributes to override the editor GUI for the component.

In the code, I used multiple custom attributes including `TitleAttribute`, `CommentAttribute`, and `CollapsedEventAttribute`. Together they create the custom editor shown in Figure 7-4 without a custom `Editor` class. I will explain `TitleAttribute` and its respective `PropertyDrawer` in the section after as an example.

Listing 7-3. SongManager (Figure 7-4) Code in Rhythm Game Starter

```
namespace RhythmGameStarter
{
    [HelpURL("https://bennykok.gitbook.io/rhythm-game-starter/
    hierarchy-overview/song-manager")]
    [RequireComponent(typeof(TrackManager))]
    public class SongManager : MonoBehaviour
    {
        [Comment("Responsible for song control, handling...")]
        public AudioSource audioSource;

        [Title("Properties", 0)]
        [Space]
        public bool playOnAwake = true;

        [Tooltip("Automatically handle play/pause when
        timescale...")]
        public bool autoTimeScalePause;
```

```
[Title("Display", 0)]
public bool progressAsPercentage = true;
public bool inverseProgressFill = false;

[Title("Events", 0)]
[CollapsedEvent("Triggered every frame when a
song progress")]
public FloatEvent onSongProgress;
[CollapsedEvent("Triggered every frame when ...")]
public FloatEvent onSongProgressFill;
    }
}
```

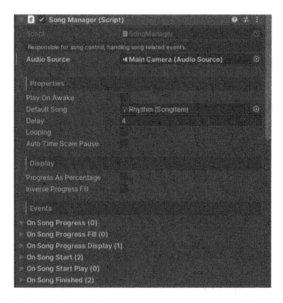

Figure 7-4. *Rhythm Game Starter's component editor using a custom PropertyDrawer*

By using the same custom attribute, I can share the custom GUI across different components easily. As shown in Figure 7-5, the `TitleAttribute` is used in other components.

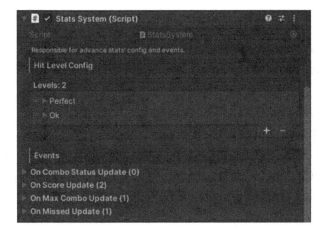

Figure 7-5. *Other components using the custom PropertyDrawer without a custom editor*

Now I will talk about the TitleAttribute mentioned above and its respective DecoratorDrawer used in Rhythm Game Starter (Listing 7-4). In this case, I used a DecoratorDrawer instead of a PropertyDrawer since the title was just a decoration to the original property so I could keep the original property GUI.

In the code, there are two classes, TitleAttribute and TitleAttributeDrawer. TitleAttribute holds the title string and boolean to indicate whether I need some extra spacing on the top of the title. By using the Conditional attribute on the class, I can prevent the attribute from being called in runtime code, which is not needed.

For the TitleAttributeDrawer class, I cache some static styles fields for frequent access (e.g. titleStyle) and only create it for the first time in the InitStyle method if it is null. Next, to override the GetHeight method to return the height of the GUI, I add an extra 12 pixel for spacing on top. Finally, I override the OnGUI method to draw the actual GUI of the title. See Figure 7-6.

Listing 7-4. Custom TitleAttribute and DecoratorDrawer

```
[Conditional("UNITY_EDITOR")]
public class TitleAttribute : PropertyAttribute
{
    public string text;
    public bool spacingTop = true;
    public TitleAttribute(string text) => this.text = text;
    public TitleAttribute(string text, bool spacingTop) :
    this(text) => this.spacingTop = spacingTop;
}

#if UNITY_EDITOR

    [CustomPropertyDrawer(typeof(TitleAttribute))]
    public class TitleAttributeDrawer : DecoratorDrawer
    {
        private static GUIStyle titleStyle;
        private static Color backgroundColor;
        private static Color rectColor;

        private static void InitStyle()
        {
            titleStyle = new GUIStyle(EditorStyles.boldLabel);
            titleStyle.normal.textColor = EditorStyles.label.
            normal.textColor;
            titleStyle.font = EditorStyles.boldFont;
            titleStyle.stretchWidth = true;
            titleStyle.padding = new RectOffset(6, 4, 4, 4);

            backgroundColor = EditorGUIUtility.isProSkin ?
            new Color(30 / 255f, 30 / 255f, 30 / 255f) : new
            Color(1f, 1f, 1f);
            backgroundColor.a = 0.3f;
```

```
        rectColor = titleStyle.normal.textColor;
        rectColor.a = 0.5f;
    }

    public override float GetHeight()
    {
        if (titleStyle == null) InitStyle();

        var titleAttribute = attribute as TitleAttribute;
        if (titleAttribute == null) return base.GetHeight();

        var height = titleStyle.CalcHeight(new
        GUIContent(titleAttribute.text), EditorGUIUtility.
        currentViewWidth);
        height += 4;
        if (titleAttribute.spacingTop)
            height += 12;

        return height;
    }

    public override void OnGUI(Rect position)
    {
        if (titleStyle == null) InitStyle();

        var titleAttribute = attribute as TitleAttribute;
        if (titleAttribute == null) return;

        position.height -= 4;
        if (titleAttribute.spacingTop)
        {
            position.y += 12;
            position.height -= 12;
        }
```

```
            var rect = new Rect(position);
            rect.width = 2;
            EditorGUI.DrawRect(rect, rectColor);

            var rect2 = new Rect(position);
            rect2.y += rect2.height;
            rect2.height = 1;
            EditorGUI.DrawRect(rect2, new Color(0, 0, 0, 0.15f));

            position.x += 2;
            position.width -= 2;
            EditorGUI.DrawRect(position, backgroundColor);

            EditorGUI.LabelField(position, titleAttribute.text,
            titleStyle);
        }
    }
#endif
```

Figure 7-6. *The custom TitleAttribute used in Rhythm Game Starter*

Custom Sequence Editor

Since the original workflow of using the asset require a MIDI file for the note sequence, which might deter people who don't know about music production or MIDI files, I thought about making a little sequencer that worked out of the box in Unity to create the note sequence. The Sequence Editor's EditorWindow (Figure 7-7) was roughly drafted within a few days and slowly fine-tuned in subsequent updates to the asset.

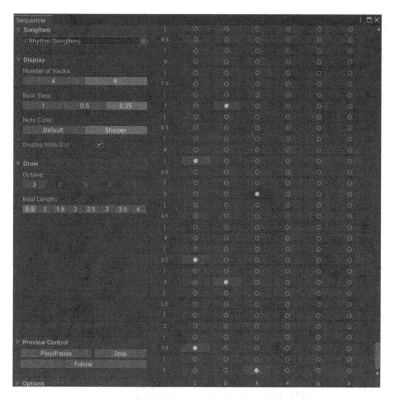

Figure 7-7. *Sequencer in Rhythm Gamer Starter*

It would be overwhelming to walk you through the whole editor code, but Listing 7-5 shows a brief overview to outline how the sequencer is structured with the side panel. You can see that complex layout with IMGUI is actually not very difficult.

In the code, I wrap the side panel and the sequencer window under a horizontal layout by using the `GUILayout.MinWidth(280)` so I can limit the width of the side panel. Next, I use a vertical layout to draw the side panel's contents vertically. Lastly, I draw out the sequencer content after the side panel.

Listing 7-5. Overview of SequenceEditor

```
namespace RhythmGameStarter
{
    public class SequenceEditor : EditorWindow
    {
        private void OnGUI()
        {
            EditorGUILayout.BeginHorizontal();
            // The sidebar layout
            EditorGUILayout.BeginVertical(GUILayout.
            MinWidth(280));
            // Drawing out the options sidebar
            //
            // Foldout
            //  └── Draw each option's section
            //
            // ... Draw other sections
            EditorGUILayout.EndVertical();

            // if we had a target song item, we draw the
               sequencer
            if (songItem) DrawSequencer();

            EditorGUILayout.EndHorizontal();
        }

        private void DrawSequencer()
        {
            // Draw through each track and each note button
            //
```

```
// Scroll View
//  └── Begin Vertical
//        └── Loop through each column
//              └── Draw each step for each column
    }
  }
}
```

The sequencer code is not included in the source repo for this chapter. Every asset's needs are different. This is a very special case that needed a custom sequencer in Unity.

Onboarding Experience

Another part of Rhythm Game Starter worth sharing is the onboarding experience. There is a Wizard window (Figure 7-8) that contains various sections to get the user started easier. Most of the time users don't read the documentation first. So if they bump into unexpected issues and a bad experience, having a welcome window like this is good for pointing them in a helpful direction. It's not necessary for all assets.

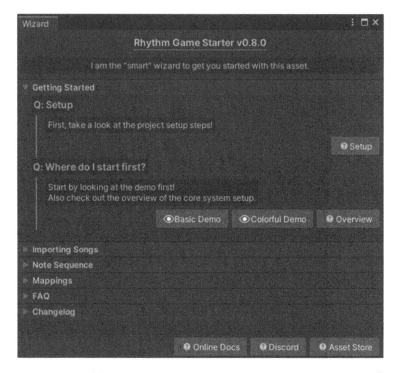

Figure 7-8. *The Welcome wizard window of Rhythm Game Starter*

The wizard displays a Q&A section about the primary features of the asset. It also opens the online documentation directly and has action buttons to highlight folders or assets in the project window to guide users to specific files.

To make the data editing easier, the wizard's data is stored in a ScriptableObject, and it also has a custom editor for editing the data (Figures 7-9 and 7-10), It might seem overly complicated, but it makes adding new sections to the Wizard window much easier.

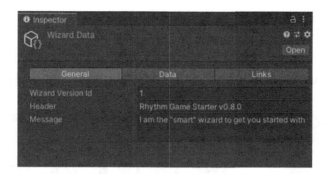

Figure 7-9. *Custom editor to edit the welcome wizard's data*

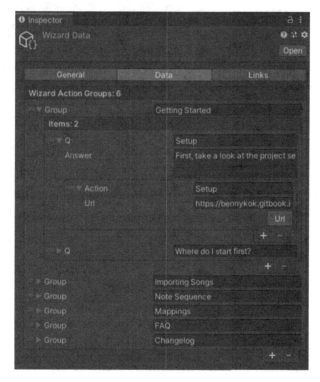

Figure 7-10. *Nested reorderableList in the editor*

Prerelease Preparation

Similar to how I prepared for the ProArray release, I prepared the screenshots, cover images, and icons using **Affinity Designer** (Figure 7-11).

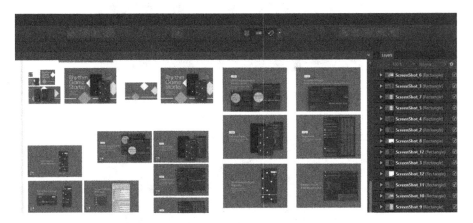

Figure 7-11. *Editing screenshots with Affinity Designer*

For the user manual, I did an online manual with **GitBook** (Figure 7-12), which has many advantages such as it's easier to update the manual right in the browser and it has more styling options. Having the online manual enables users to view the documentation details of your asset before they purchase it, so they can understand how your asset works and see if it really fits their needs beforehand.

GitBook is an online service that lets you create and edit your documentation site with its online editor and deploy your site automatically under its domain. If you use the personal plan, you can do the job without many limitations. For more details about setting up an online documentation site, read the following chapters.

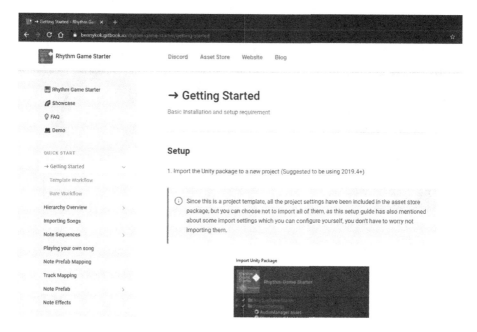

Figure 7-12. *Rhythm Game Starter's GitBook documentation*

Post-Release Analysis

After the release of Rhythm Game Starter, I linked my **Google Analytics** account to my publisher account, which provides insights to the asset page's analytics. In Figure 7-13, you can see that most of the page view is for the package ID 160117, which is the Rhythm Game Starter package, and most of the users were either from Japan or US, showing that the rhythm game genre is more popular in these areas, which could possibly explain why this became the best performing asset due to the popularity of the rhythm game genre.

Figure 7-13. *Google Analytics page linked to my publisher account*

Figure 7-14 and Table 7-1 show the revenue graph from the initial release in January 2020 to February 2021. The monthly net revenue ranged from $200 to $600 USD, with highest peak around $900 USD, as you can see from the graph. Most of the revenue spikes can be attributed to official Asset Store sales. Usually selected assets are 30 to 50% off, which is a great deal; this doubled the amount of purchases most of the time. I was lucky to have Rhythm Game Starter in those special sales. The first sale I was in mostly featuring new assets, and it's way easier for users to spot the discounted Rhythm Game Starter.

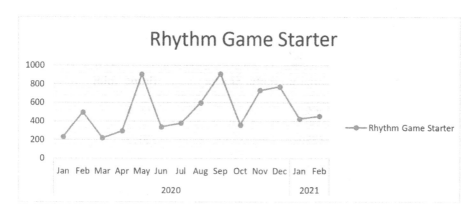

Figure 7-14. *Net revenue trend of Rhythm Game Starter from January 2020 to February 2021*

Table 7-1. *Net Revenue Table of Rhythm Game Starter from January 2020 to February 2021*

Sum of Net	Product	
Date	Rhythm Game Starter	Grand Total
2020	6230	6230
Jan	231	231
Feb	495.6	495.6
Mar	218.4	218.4
Apr	294	294
May	905.1	905.1
Jun	338.1	338.1
Jul	378	378
Aug	598.5	598.5
Sep	909.3	909.3

(*continued*)

Table 7-1. (*continued*)

Sum of Net	Product	
Date	Rhythm Game Starter	Grand Total
Oct	359.1	359.1
Nov	731.5	731.5
Dec	771.4	771.4
2021	877.8	877.8
Jan	425.6	425.6
Feb	452.2	452.2
Grand Total	7107.8	7107.8

Comparing the charts of the two assets, you can obviously see the difference, with Rhythm Game Starter leading (Figure 7-15).

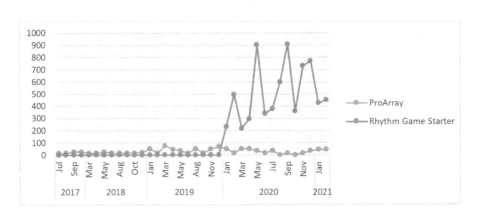

Figure 7-15. *Net revenue comparison of ProArray and Rhythm Game Starter from July 2017 to February 2021*

To provide instant asset support, I usually provide a link to a Discord server (Figure 7-16) in the asset store page description so users can reach out to me directly. Having a Discord server is a great way to grow the community around your assets.

If you do not know about Discord, it is a cross-platform instant messaging app. It allows you to create a private space where you can invite people into your own community, called a server. You can learn more about Discord on the official website at `https://discord.com/`.

Figure 7-16. *Discord support server*

Summary

Releasing Rhythm Game Starter within a short period of time and having it perform way better than ProArray was unexpected. The timing and opportunities were right on time. I was stoked at that moment.

In its first month of release, Rhythm Game Starter generated $231 USD in passive income for me with 11 purchases. Then it appeared in the "Top New" section of the Assets Store, and for the rest of 2020 it was continuously included in official sales on the Unity Assets Store. This totally changed my view of asset publishing.

Looking back at the previous year (2020, which was a weird year already with all the things happening around the world), it is hard to differentiate which major factors contributed to Rhythm Game Starter's result. However, the market has obviously shown that Rhythm Game Starter is more popular than ProArray.

By further comparing the two assets, both are in a niche area. At the time, there weren't many similar assets available. What's left on the table is that Rhythm Game Starter targets an wider range of audience. The rhythm game is a well-established game genre like platformer, first person shooter, etc., so it's easier to attract people who want to make similar types of games organically. On the other hand, ProArray doesn't stand out from the sea of assets. If we consider ProArray as a level design tool, there are many options to compete with. Therefore, ProArray's position in the marketplace is not clear enough for people to see the unique values in it, whereas Rhythm Game Starter is easy to spot as a game template. It lives in a niche area with a strong community, that of rhythm games.

> You can't connect the dots looking forward; you can only connect them looking backwards. So you have to trust that the dots will somehow connect in your future...
>
> — Steve Jobs

One thing I am certain about is that my experience with ProArray and the other free assets really contributed to the success of Rhythm Game Starter. I think it is much more worthwhile than it seems to spend almost five years working on and updating an asset that doesn't get a lot of attention. I believe it is one the dots that connects forward, and I sharpened my skill set on every aspect with Unity along the way. So don't get down on yourself too soon, and keep hustling.

Let's move on now. Next I will talk about the asset publishing workflow and distribution on Unity's Assets Store or open source on GitHub!

## CHAPTER 8

Asset Workflow for Publishing

In this chapter, I will cover efficient workflows for developing Unity assets and packages with version control and a modular structure. I will walk you through installing **Git** on your local machine and setting it up with your Unity projects in various ways. I will also cover basic ways of using Git commands and Git GUI clients to commit and push to a remote repository.

Next, I will talk about using **standard-version** to automate package versioning and changelog generation, which can save you time with iterative assets or package updates.

Finally, I will talk about two ways of setting up online documentation: with **GitBook**, an easy-to-use online documentation builder, or manually with **DocFX,** which you can use to generate source code documentation from your C# project. I will also talk about how to customize your DocFX site and host it with **Netlify**.

Version Control with Git

The most important thing in software development is version control. I assume most of you reading this book already know about version control. Simply put, it's a systems that allows a software developer to track changes in a repository and lets you roll back to an older version any time. **Git**

© Benny Kok 2021
B. Kok, *Beginning Unity Editor Scripting*, https://doi.org/10.1007/978-1-4842-7167-4_8

is a popular choice among other options available, such as Subversion and PlasticSCM. The latter have advantages compared to Git, but in my opinion, at the end of the day, Git has the strongest community, and with platforms like **GitHub** and **GitLab** available freely for you to host a remote Git repository, it is the way to go! It is very easy to understand the concept of other version control systems once you get the gist of Git, no pun intended.

Do You Git?

In this section, I will assume you are new to Git. I will go through setting up a local Git repository step by step, but feel free to skip ahead to the section about .gitignore or LFS if you already know Git.

First, you must install Git locally on your working machine. Head over to `https://git-scm.com/` and download the latest Git executable for your OS.

Next, open up your terminal of choice and test if Git is installed properly by typing in `git version` to check for the Git version:

```
C:\Users\kokbe>git version
git version 2.23.0.windows.1
```

If you encounter some issues like `'git'` is not recognized as an `internal` or `external command`, please check if the Git's executable folder is in the environment variable path.

Git init

Now it's time to create a local Git repository in your Unity project folder. There are many ways to help you create a local Git repository, but the most direct way is to use Git via the command line. A quick way to open up the command line on Windows is by typing `cmd` in the file explorer (Figure 8-1). Next, type `git init` in the terminal and your Git repo will be created.

Figure 8-1. *By typing cmd in the path of the Windows Explorer you can open cmd at that path*

```
C:\Users\kokbe\Documents\GitHub\TestGit>git init
Initialized empty Git repository in C:/Users/kokbe/Documents/
GitHub/TestGit/.git/
```

After running the command, you will see that the `.git` folder has been created (Figure 8-2).

Figure 8-2. *The .git folder created by Git*

If you can't see it on Windows, you will need turn on the Show hidden files option in the File Explorer options (Figure 8-3).

Figure 8-3. *Turning on the Show hidden files option*

Once you have the Git repository initialized, you can type in git status to check the status of the local Git repo:

```
C:\Users\kokbe\Documents\GitHub\TestGit>git status
On branch master

No commits yet

Untracked files:
  (use "git add <file>..." to include in what will be committed)
        .vscode/
        Assets/
        Library/
        Logs/
        Packages/
        ProjectSettings/
        Temp/
        TestGit.sln

nothing added to commit but untracked files present (use "git
add" to track)
```

Before doing your first commit, there are some extra things that need to be set up, like .gitignore and Git LFS (large file storage). I will talk about them in the following two sections. Alternative, if you use the GitHub Unity Plugin (https://unity.github.com/) which has an in-editor experience for setting up a local Git repository, it will handle git init, .gitignore, and LFS for Unity. But by doing it all manually you get to be more flexible and can learn more about Git.

Git Ignore

Most of the time Git doesn't need to keep track of all of the folders and files, since they might be either automatically generated or just cache files.

In Unity's case, the Library folder is simply a cache folder for Unity to cache all the editor-generated resource, such as compiled scripts' DLLs, compiled shader cache, etc. Usually the Library folder is very large and can be generated again anytime. That's where the .gitignore file comes into play: Git will ignore tracking the files, folders, and patterns listed in this file.

To get started with a Unity-specific .gitignore template, head over to https://github.com/github/gitignore where you can find almost any .gitignore template you can think of. This is what a .gitignore file will look like:

```
# This .gitignore file should be placed at the root of your
Unity project directory
#
# Get latest from https://github.com/github/gitignore/blob/
master/Unity.gitignore
#
/[Ll]ibrary/
/[Tt]emp/
/[Oo]bj/
/[Bb]uild/
/[Bb]uilds/
/[Ll]ogs/
/[Uu]ser[Ss]ettings/

# MemoryCaptures can get excessive in size.
# They also could contain extremely sensitive data
/[Mm]emoryCaptures/
...
```

However, copying and pasting the .gitignore file every time you set up a new local Git repository is troublesome, so here is a pro tip for you. First you must install **Node.js** by heading over to https://nodejs.org/

and downloading Node.js for your machine. Node.js provides a JavaScript runtime environment on your machine. By installing it, you get access to the npm and npx commands, which are the Node Package Manager commands. They usually work with web development. npm is used to manage the dependencies used by your web project and npx lets you execute npm packages without installing them. So with Node.js installed you can execute some utility tools that will simplify adding the .gitignore file for you in command line.

There is a neat npm package called add-gitignore by Tejas Kumar from www.npmjs.com/package/add-gitignore that lets you search (Figure 8-4) and add a .gitignore template (Figure 8-5) by just running a command in your target directory. You can do so by typing npx add-gitignore:

```
C:\Users\kokbe\Documents\GitHub\TestGit>npx add-gitignore
```

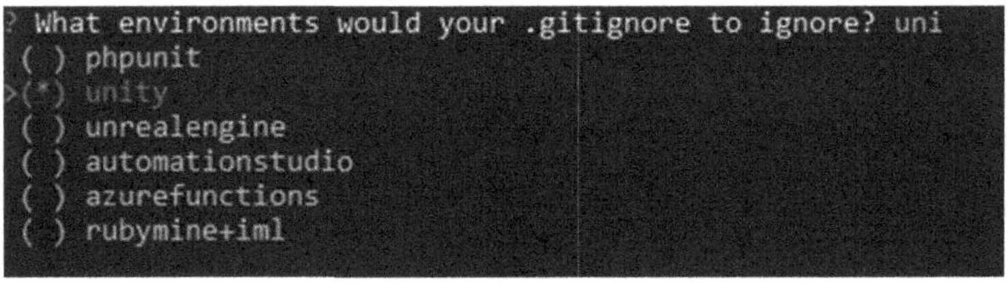

Figure 8-4. *Search and press space to select the .gitignore template*

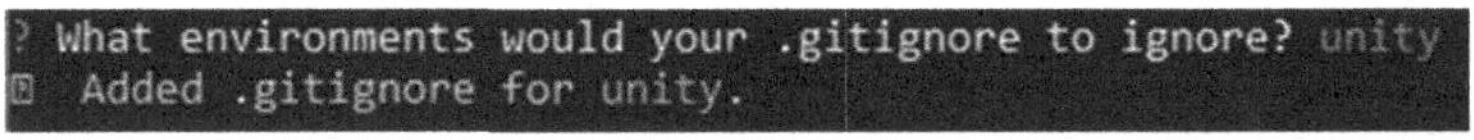

Figure 8-5. *Press Enter to confirm adding the selected .gitignore template*

Under the hood, this package pulls the .gitignore file from www.gitignore.io.

Git LFS

Now, let's talk about Git LFS. LFS replaces large files in your remote Git repo with text pointers and stores those files in a separate space, which can reduce the remote core repo's size while still keeping track of your large file versions. Using LFS with Unity projects is very common and most Git providers like GitHub and GitLab already support LFS.

For most lightweight Unity projects, the large storage of GitHub's repository should be enough. However, if your project starts to grow, be aware about the large storage limitation.

From the GitHub docs: "We recommend repositories remain small, ideally less than 1GB, and less than 5GB is strongly recommended." [1] With the GitHub Free plan, currently you can only have around 1GB max size if you are using LFS. With GitLab, you can have up to 10GB per repo at the time this book was written.

While both services are free to use (plus paid advance features), I switched to GitLab for most of my newer personal Unity projects to take advantage of the larger file storage, while most open source small utility projects go to GitHub.

Using LFS will generally be faster in cloning and fetching files from your remote compared to repositories without using LFS. To set up LFS, it requires a separate download of the LFS executable from https://git-lfs.github.com/. After installing, you need to call a few commands in your project directory to set it up:

```
C:\Users\kokbe\Documents\GitHub\TestGit>git lfs install
Updated git hooks.
Git LFS initialized.
```

---

[1] https://docs.github.com/en/github/managing-large-files/what-is-my-disk-quota

To configure which file type Git LFS should be tracking, you need to use the `track` command with the type of file you want LFS to track. Afterwards, you can see that a `.gitattributes` was created (Figure 8-6).

```
C:\Users\kokbe\Documents\GitHub\TestGit>git lfs track "*.prefab"
Tracking "*.prefab"
```

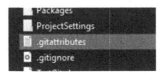

Figure 8-6. *The .gitattributesfile, which stores the LFS tracking patterns*

Hopefully you get the idea. You are not going to track every file by typing the `track` command. You can easily get the same `.gitattributes` used by the Unity GitHub Plugin from the GitHub repo, specifically at `https://github.com/github-for-unity/Unity/blob/master/src/ GitHub.Api/Resources/.gitattributes`, and then paste in the file in your project folder.

An alternative (and my favorite way) is to use my little npm package named add-unitylfs from `www.npmjs.com/package/add-unitylfs`. Similar to `add-gitignore`, you type `npx add-unitylfs`:

```
C:\Users\kokbe\Documents\GitHub\TestGit>npx add-unitylfs
.gitattributes was Added!
stdout: Updated git hooks.
Git LFS initialized.
```

Git Client

Now that you have your local repo set up with `.gitignore` and LFS, you can use a Git client to view and even publish your local repo to a remote environment directly. A few are **GitHub Desktop**, **Fork**, and **Sourcetree**. Most Git clients have an intuitive UI for the Git commands.

For GitHub Desktop, you can install it from `https://desktop.github.com/`. After installing GitHub Desktop, you can locate your local Git repo via File ➤ Add local repository (Figure 8-7).

Figure 8-7. *Locating the local Git repo*

Now you can see your local repo changes and history and you can commit directly without typing any commands (Figure 8-8).

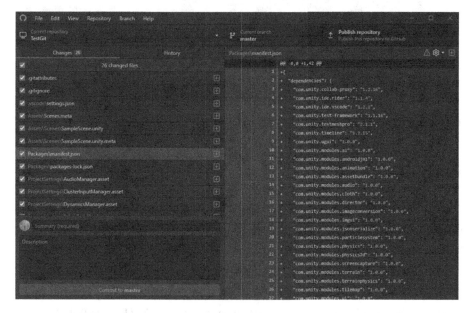

Figure 8-8. *GitHub Desktop's interface*

For Fork (Figure 8-9), which I prefer over GitHub Desktop, you can download and install it from `https://git-fork.com/`.

Fork is my daily driver since it has a tree structure view for the changed files, which makes it easier to get an overview of your local repository before a commit. Also, with its tab layout, it's easy to switch between local repos.

Figure 8-9. *Fork's interface*

Remote

Now that you have a local repository ready to go, you can create a remote repository with a remote Git provider such as GitHub and GitLab, which lets you share a public or private repository on the cloud. By doing so, your project can be easily synced up in the cloud and you can invite other collaborators. If you are using GitHub Desktop, you can easily do this by pressing the Publish repository button on the top right (Figure 8-10).

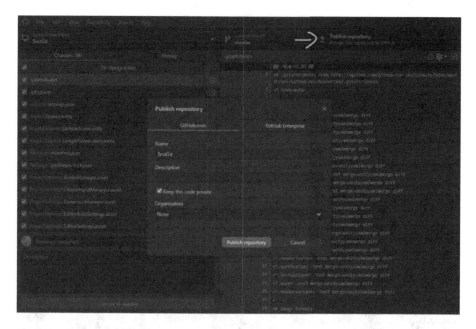

Figure 8-10. *Publishing the repo directly from GitHub Desktop*

Alternatively, you can create a repo on GitHub or GitLab first. I talk about how to use commands to link up the remote in your local repository in a later section.

When creating a repo on GitHub, you can choose between public or private (Figure 8-11).

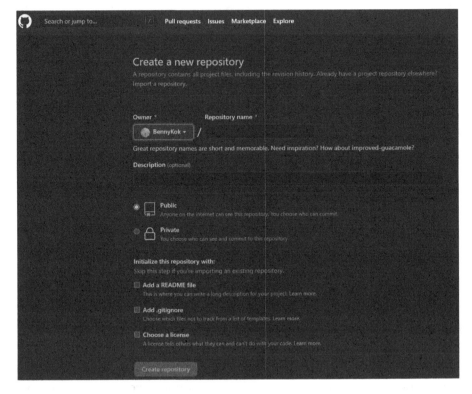

Figure 8-11. *Creating a Git repo on GitHub*

Locate the Git URL on GitHub by tapping the green Code button and copy the URL you see there (Figure 8-12).

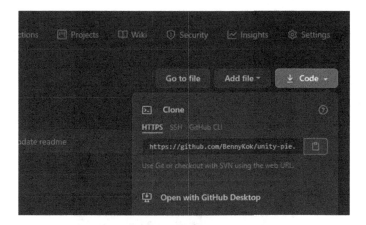

Figure 8-12. *Locating the URL in GitHub*

If you are using GitLab, the interface is similar. You can also choose
between private or public (Figure 8-13).

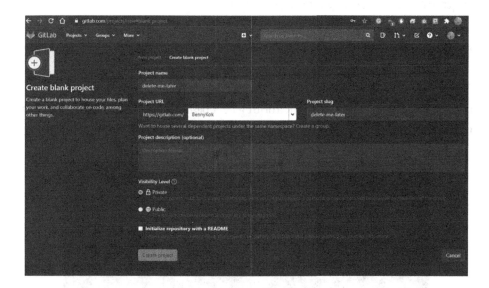

Figure 8-13. *Creating a Git repo on GitLab*

Locate the Git URL on GitLab by tapping the blue Code button and
copy the URL you see there (Figure 8-14).

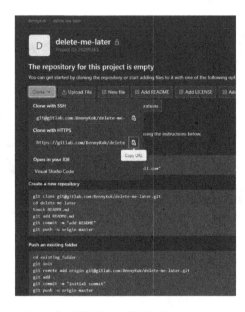

Figure 8-14. *Locating the URL in GitLab*

Commit and Push

Now that you know about creating a remote repository and have your remote Git URL ready, let's talk about git commit and how to start pushing to the remote. Let's check the git status first (Figure 8-15).

```
C:\Users\kokbe\Documents\GitHub\TestGit>git status
On branch master

No commits yet

Untracked files:
  (use "git add <file>..." to include in what will be committed)
        .gitattributes
        .gitignore
        .vscode/
        Assets/
        Packages/
        ProjectSettings/
        package-lock.json

nothing added to commit but untracked files present (use "git add" to track)
```

Figure 8-15. *Checking the git status*

To update your local changes to the remote, you have to commit first. To commit via the terminal, you must stage your changes first by typing in git add <files> to stage all files directly. I usually type in git add . as shown in Figure 8-16.

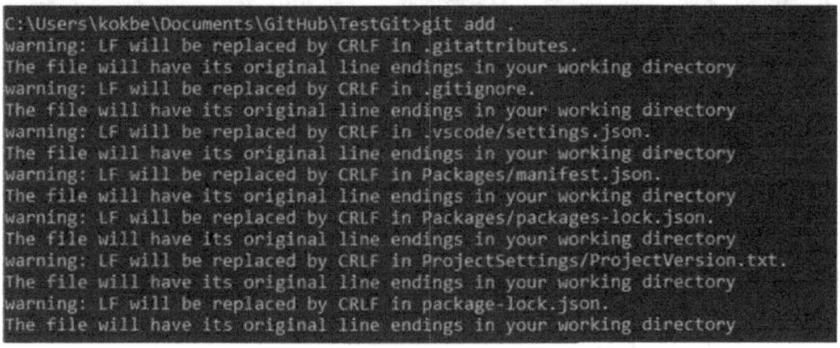

Figure 8-16. *Staging all of the files for the init commit*

You can commit with this command with a commit message of git commit -m "init commit" (Figure 8-17).

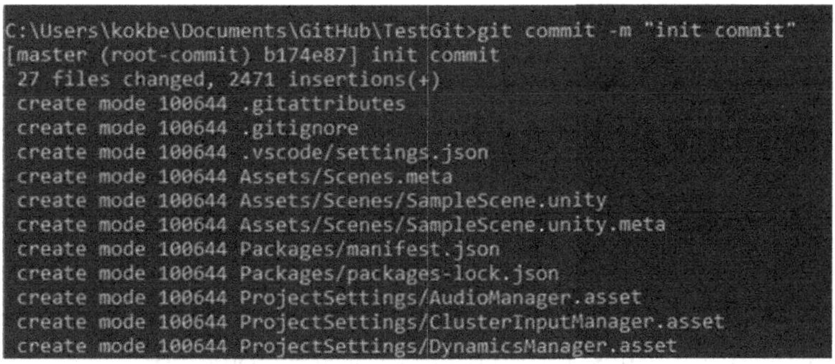

Figure 8-17. *A git commit*

Next, you can use git log to view the commit log (Figure 8-18).

```
C:\Users\kokbe\Documents\GitHub\TestGit>git log
commit b174e87d10eb62f01bb5bddcc9d7b795a38c73fb (HEAD -> master)
Author: BennyKok <itechbenny@gmail.com>
Date:   Sat Mar 20 21:15:22 2021 +0800

    init commit

C:\Users\kokbe\Documents\GitHub\TestGit>_
```

Figure 8-18. *Using the git log command to view the commit log*

To link up your local repo to the remote, you have to use the git URL that you just copied from your GitHub or GitLab page and add it as a remote next `git push -u <remote> <branch>` the first time to specify which branch to track. The first time you push to remote with a URL, your system will also prompt you to authenticate with the remote first. You will have to enter your GitHub or GitLab email and password once.

```
git remote add origin https://gitlab.com/BennyKok/delete-me-later.git
git push -u origin master
```

For a consecutive push, you can just use the `git push` command.

Submodules Are Key

With Git, there is a feature called **submodules**, which allows you to basically nest another Git repository into your current repository (Figure 8-19). This is a very powerful concept. As soon as I realized the flexibility of submodules, I used them almost everywhere.

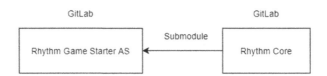

Figure 8-19. *Concept of a submodule in remote*

In my Rhythm Game Starter Project, I added the core package of the asset as a submodule in a standard Unity project. With both repositories hosted on GitLab, the submodule represents a link to the source repository (Figure 8-20).

Figure 8-20. *In the GitLab browser, a submodule represent a link to the actual repo*

For the purpose of uploading the asset to the Asset Store with different Unity versions, this allows me to synchronize the same core package in any Unity version easily for version compatibility tests and to update the core package right there in place if some Unity API changed in the new version, which unlocks a whole new world of flexibility (Figure 8-21).

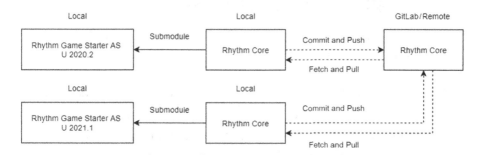

Figure 8-21. *Concept of using submodules to synchronize between a developing asset on different versions of Unity*

Moreover, with the submodule concept, now I can create and have my reusable UPM packages hosted on GitHub or GitLab, and whenever I am working on a new project, I can include them as submodules in the project's Packages folder (Figure 8-22), and UPM will recognize them as embedded local packages, which cleans up my Assets folder. The project size will also be smaller. Since I can have a centralized source for each personal package, I can update each of the packages right in every project and synchronize the changes back to other projects that use the same packages.

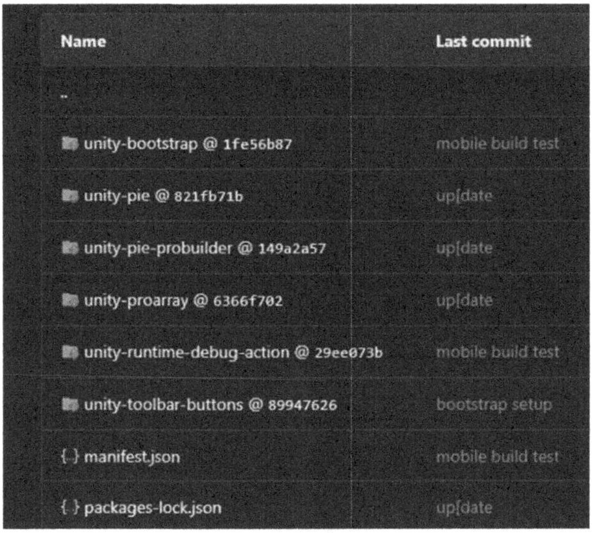

Figure 8-22. *Adding UPM-compatible packages as submodules in the Packages directory*

To add a submodule to your existing repo, in your target directory run git submodule add <remote_url> <optional_directory_name>.

So in this case, I cd into the Packages directory and then git submodule add https://github.com/BennyKok/unity-hierarchy-header.git for example to add one of my own utility packages to the project. Since this package follows the UPM package structure, it has a package.json and asmdef setup for the Runtime/Editor directory, thus UPM will treat it as a local embedded package and it will work like a normal UPM package.

Changelog and Versioning

Now that you know about setting up a local Git repository and pushing to remote, you can now manage your asset project without stress. With version control, there is no need to be afraid of losing track of changes, and you can always go back to the previous commit if you messed up something. The more you get into optimizing the workflow, the more things you do manually can be automated.

For instance, it is now possible to automate the changelog generation based on your commit messages and automate package versioning based on the commit messages type. You may have heard about semantic versioning. Currently all of Unity's official packages (Figure 8-23) use it to generate the changelog and bump the versions.

Figure 8-23. *Unity's URP package changelog*

Standard-Version

During my "research" (I Googled for a while), I found out about another similar NPM library called **standard-version** at `https://github.com/conventional-changelog/standard-version`. It uses Conventional

Commits (www.conventionalcommits.org/en/v1.0.0/), an open standard of formatting commit message for generating a changelog, which is very much the same and compatible with the semantic versioning format, and it appears to me that the documentation for standard-version is more upfront and flexible to use.

I used standard-version in one of my latest asset projects and it saved me tons of time by not needing to update the changelog every time for a new release. By following the commit format (Figure 8-24) suggested in Conventional Commits, the generated changelog will automatically group the messages into different sections for you. With standard-version (using conventional changelog under the hood) it detects different commit message types and categorizes them, such as a commit message with a "fix:" prefix.

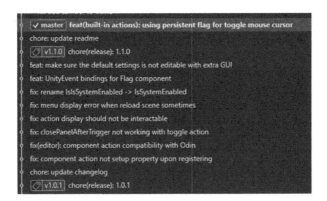

Figure 8-24. *Commit message of my Runtime Debug Action asset*

The fix "action display should not be intractable" will be in the Bug Fixes group in the generated changelog file (Figure 8-25).

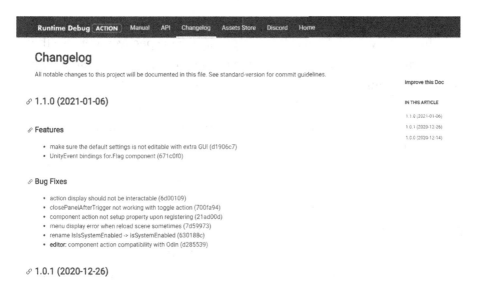

Figure 8-25. *Generated changelog[2] of my Runtime Debug Action asset*

For some common commit message prefixes, you can take a look at Table 8-1.

Table 8-1. *Common Conventional Commit Message Prefixes*

Commit Message Prefix	Usage	Changelog Section
`fix:`	For bug fixes	Bug Fixes
`feat:`	For added features	Features
`refactor:`	For refactoring-related changes	Refactor
`chore:`	For changes that don't really fit into bug fixes or features and will not appear in the changelog	N/A
`docs:`	For documentation-related changes; will not appear in the changelog	N/A

---

[2]https://bennykok.github.io/runtime-debug-action-docs/CHANGELOG.html

The table just goes through the common commit message types that I most frequently used. For each prefix you also can specify a scope so that the commit can be more specific, such as `fix(core): fix` for a small bug in the core module.

For more details about the commit message's prefix standards, please take a look at the Conventional Commit site at `www.conventionalcommits.org/en/v1.0.0/`.

Using standard-version

There are multiple ways to execute the standard-version package. I installed it globally by running `npm i -g standard-version` in my terminal. Next, make sure you have a `package.json` file in your project directory. This works the best if you are working on a UPM package because you will already have a `package.json`. However, you can have a `package.json` even if you are on a normal asset project because it's still very useful to keep track of the package information (e.g. version, author), and it will be easier for you to transition your project to a UPM-compatible one by adding the correct metadata in the future.

To quickly create a package.json file, use the `npm init` command. You can remove any unused fields later (Figure 8-26).

```
C:\Users\kokbe\Documents\GitHub\TestGit>npm init
This utility will walk you through creating a package.json file.
It only covers the most common items, and tries to guess sensible defaults.

See `npm help init` for definitive documentation on these fields
and exactly what they do.

Use `npm install <pkg>` afterwards to install a package and
save it as a dependency in the package.json file.

Press ^C at any time to quit.
package name: (testgit)
version: (1.0.0)
description:
```

Figure 8-26. *Using npm init to create a package.json file faster*

The first time you generate the changelog, run `standard-version` `--first-release` in your terminal so that it will not bump your package version. After running standard-version, it will automatically tag a git release so that it can track the commit messages between for the next changelog generation. If you are not sure about the changelog generation, you can run `standard-version --dry-run`, and it will only display the version bump and changelog preview in the terminal while not affecting your files (Figure 8-27).

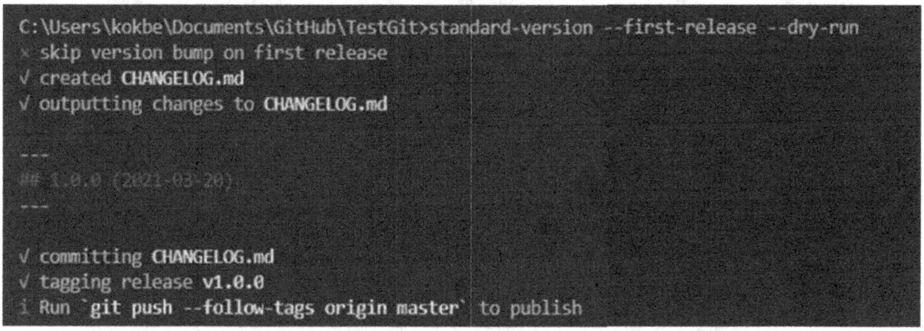

```
C:\Users\kokbe\Documents\GitHub\TestGit>standard-version --first-release --dry-run
× skip version bump on first release
√ created CHANGELOG.md
√ outputting changes to CHANGELOG.md

---
## 1.0.0 (2021-03-20)
---

√ committing CHANGELOG.md
√ tagging release v1.0.0
i Run `git push --follow-tags origin master` to publish
```

Figure 8-27. *Running with --first-release and --dry-run flag*

Now, let's try staging some files and committing them (Figure 8-28).

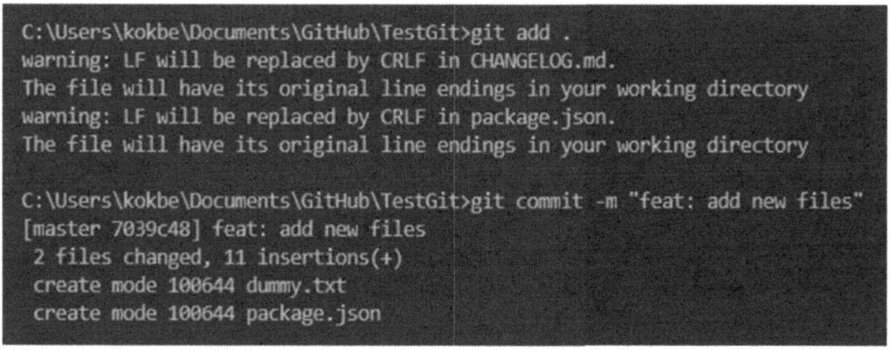

```
C:\Users\kokbe\Documents\GitHub\TestGit>git add .
warning: LF will be replaced by CRLF in CHANGELOG.md.
The file will have its original line endings in your working directory
warning: LF will be replaced by CRLF in package.json.
The file will have its original line endings in your working directory

C:\Users\kokbe\Documents\GitHub\TestGit>git commit -m "feat: add new files"
[master 7039c48] feat: add new files
 2 files changed, 11 insertions(+)
 create mode 100644 dummy.txt
 create mode 100644 package.json
```

Figure 8-28. *Staging the files and committing them*

205

Tip   NPM packages like **commitizen** make it easier for you to add a commit message prefix by providing a list of options in the command line for you to choose directly.

Now let's run through standard-version and see how it generates the changelog (Figure 8-29) and bumps the version in action.

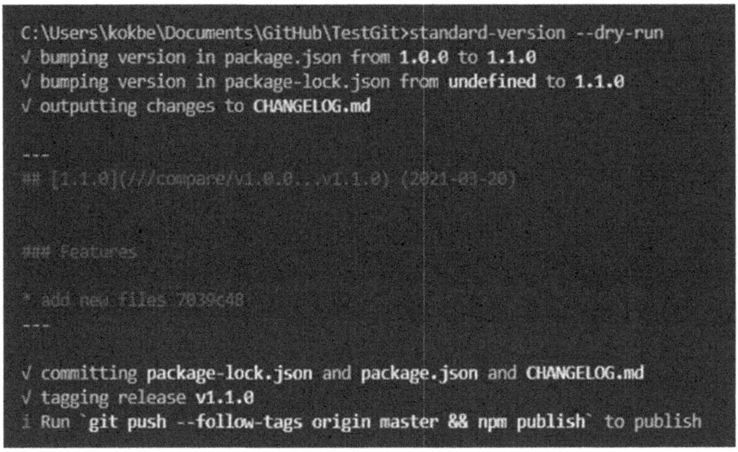

```
C:\Users\kokbe\Documents\GitHub\TestGit>standard-version --dry-run
√ bumping version in package.json from 1.0.0 to 1.1.0
√ bumping version in package-lock.json from undefined to 1.1.0
√ outputting changes to CHANGELOG.md

---

## [1.1.0](///compare/v1.0.0...v1.1.0) (2021-03-20)


### Features

* add new files 7039c48

---

√ committing package-lock.json and package.json and CHANGELOG.md
√ tagging release v1.1.0
i Run `git push --follow-tags origin master && npm publish` to publish
```

Figure 8-29. *Dry running standard-version*

Lastly, you can preview the changelog file in VS code by using the shortcut Ctrl + k + v (Figure 8-30).

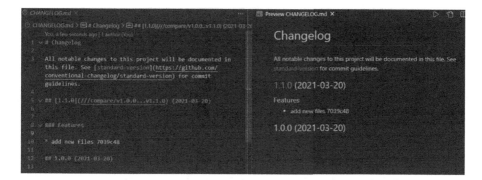

Figure 8-30. *Previewing the md file in VS code, (Ctrl + k + v)*

Documentation

You should have an idea of how to use **Git** for version control and use **standard-version** for changelog and version automation for your asset package. It's time to talk about the documentation for your asset. I will go through two solutions, **GitBook** and **DocFX**. GitBook is intuitive to use; you can publish to the web in a second. DocFX requires some manual setup, but it can generate source documentation from your C# codebase, which is a big advantage if your asset or package is more towards the scripting side of Unity.

GitBook

GitBook is a free-to-use online service with paid plans for more advanced features, but the personal plan is enough for most small and medium online documentation.

Creating a Space

You start by creating an account on GitBook. GitBook offers a WYSIWYG (what-you-see-is-what-you-get) experience. First you need to create a space for your documentation (Figure 8-31).

Figure 8-31. *GitBook's main dashboard where you can create a space*

Editing Content

Over on the left navigation panel (Figure 8-32), you can add pages, groups, external links, and even import a page from other sources.

Figure 8-32. *Adding pages, groups, and links, and importing*

You can add a different card by clicking the plus button at the left corner or between each element (Figure 8-33).

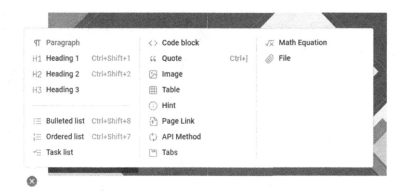

Figure 8-33. *Available card to add*

You can format text easily (Figure 8-34).

Overview

RhythmGameStarter is a rhythm game starter template [B I S | <>] midi workflow that supports importing midi files, now also has a sequence editor to create any sequence from scratch.

In runtime, each note in the sequence is mapped to different note prefab types for different interactions (Tap, Long Press, Swipe), notes' transform will be synchronized with the music playing. The asset also comes with a simple stats system with combos, scores, etc...

⚠ For version 0.3.0+, will only support 2019.4 LTS+

Figure 8-34. *Text editing and formatting*

By pasting a YouTube link, GitBook will help you create a YouTube Player embed (Figure 8-35) for it directly, so you can also include your tutorial videos on the site.

Figure 8-35. *Embedded YouTube player*

Wrapping Up

When you are ready, save and merge your changes, and the changes will be live immediately (Figure 8-36).

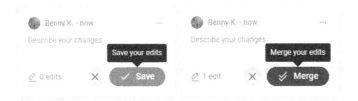

Figure 8-36. *Save and merge your changes so they will go live*

Then you can find the shareable link (Figure 8-37) and include it on your Asset Store page.

Figure 8-37. *The shareable link of your GitBook page*

For reference, you can take a look at my GitBook pages for Rhythm Game Starter at `https://bennykok.gitbook.io/rhythm-game-starter/` (Figure 8-38).

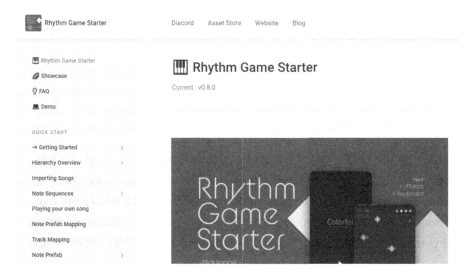

Figure 8-38. *Rhythm Game Starter's GitBook pages*

DocFX

DocFX is a powerful static documentation generator that is specifically made for .NET languages by Microsoft. It also supports languages like Java, Python, and TypeScript. In this case, it will work perfectly and generate a working static documentation website from a Unity C# project.

Start by installing DocFX. You'll use the Object Spawner tool from a previous chapter and generate documentation for it. Then you'll host it online with **Netlify**.

Installing DocFX

To install DocFX, you must download the DocFX CLI tools. There are two ways: install them via a package manager or download the executable directly from the GitHub repo release page.

On Windows, you first need to install the Chocolatey package manager from `https://chocolatey.org/install`. If you are on a Mac, DocFX is also available on Homebrew at `https://formulae.brew.sh/formula/docfx`. Run this command afterwards:

```
// On Windows
choco install docfx
// On Mac
brew install docfx
```

Setting Up a DocFX Project

Next, using the Object Spawner tool examples from a previous chapter, you can set up a DocFX project to generating docs for it. Since you created asmdef for both the editor and runtime scripts for it, Unity will generate the `.csproj` file needed for DocFX to generate documentation, and you will put the DocFX project in your Unity project's root directory (Figure 8-39).

Figure 8-39. *The Object Spawner tool structure*

In the root directory of your Unity Project, run the docfx init -q command to set up the DocFX project (Figure 8-40).

```
Hub\Beginning Unity Editor Scripting>docfx init -q
\Documents\GitHub\Beginning Unity Editor Scripting\docfx_project\src
\Documents\GitHub\Beginning Unity Editor Scripting\docfx_project\api
\Documents\GitHub\Beginning Unity Editor Scripting\docfx_project\apidoc
\Documents\GitHub\Beginning Unity Editor Scripting\docfx_project\articles
\Documents\GitHub\Beginning Unity Editor Scripting\docfx_project\images
Documents\GitHub\Beginning Unity Editor Scripting\docfx_project\toc.yml
Documents\GitHub\Beginning Unity Editor Scripting\docfx_project\index.md
Documents\GitHub\Beginning Unity Editor Scripting\docfx_project\api\toc.yml
Documents\GitHub\Beginning Unity Editor Scripting\docfx_project\api\index.md
Documents\GitHub\Beginning Unity Editor Scripting\docfx_project\articles\toc.ym
Documents\GitHub\Beginning Unity Editor Scripting\docfx_project\articles\intro.
Documents\GitHub\Beginning Unity Editor Scripting\docfx_project\.gitignore
Documents\GitHub\Beginning Unity Editor Scripting\docfx_project\api\.gitignore
\kokbe\Documents\GitHub\Beginning Unity Editor Scripting\docfx_project\docfx.js
t docfx project to C:\Users\kokbe\Documents\GitHub\Beginning Unity Editor Scri
```

Figure 8-40. *Running the docfx init command*

You will see the docfx_project directory being created. The docfx. json is the configuration file you can modify and set as the path to point to the .csproj in your Unity project, so that when you call the docfx command, it knows where to look for your C# classes. Let's head over to docfx.json and modify the src field to point to its parent directory and list the target .csproj file related to your tool project only (Figure 8-41).

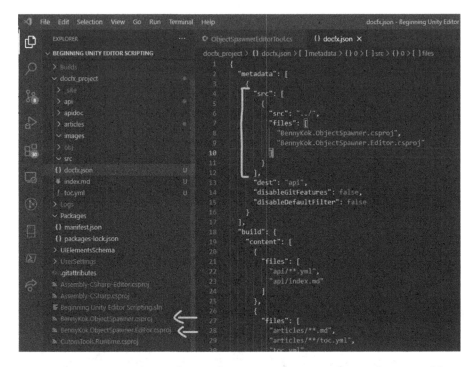

Figure 8-41. *Setting up the path to point to your desired .csproj file*

To build and serve the docfx site locally, run `docfx --serve` in your terminal (Figure 8-42).

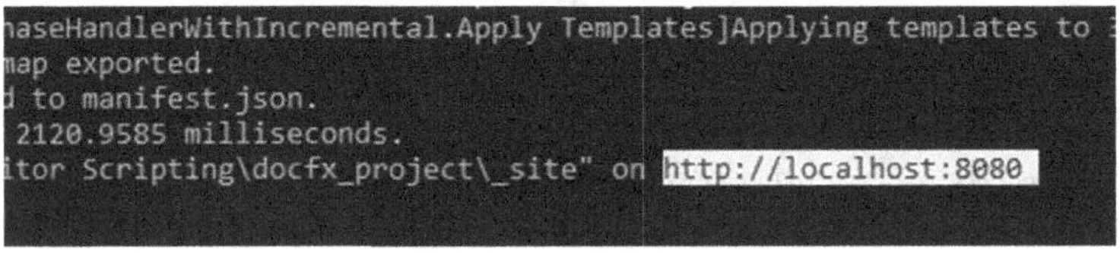

Figure 8-42. *After running docfx --serve, make sure to keep the terminal running to keep serving the site*

By default, the site will be served on `http://localhost:8080`. Voilà! You have a static site generated with all of your namespaces, classes, fields, and methods detailed if you head over to the API Documentation tab (Figure 8-43).

Figure 8-43. *Generated API docs*

C# Code Documentation

Now that the site can be generated from your source code, you can add extra comments and descriptions for fields and method parameters in the source code and let DocFX include them in the generated site. Let's jump back into the Unity project for the Object Spawner tool.

To facilitate the formatting of the code comments, a VS code extension is suggested (Figure 8-44).

Figure 8-44. *C# XML Documentation Comments helper extension*

This will help you quickly scaffold the standard C# XML documentation comments by typing three slashes, /// (Figure 8-45).

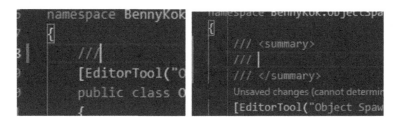

Figure 8-45. *Typing /// above a class will generate the summary XML tag*

After you have filled in the summary about the class (Figure 8-46), rerun the docfx --serve command and see the regenerated site (Figure 8-47).

Figure 8-46. *Filling in the summary for the class*

Figure 8-47. *The summary will appear in the generated docs*

If it doesn't reflect your changes from your code, try regenerating the `.csproj` file in Unity via Edit ➤ Preference ➤ External Tools ➤ Regenerate project files (Figure 8-48).

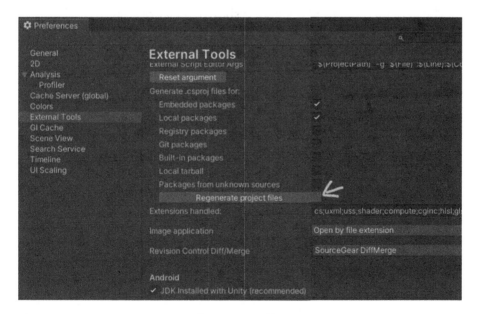

Figure 8-48. *Regenerating the .csproj file*

If you type /// above a method, it will automatically generate the summary and param tag for each of the parameters (Figure 8-49).

```
/// <summary>
///          You, a few seconds ago • Uncommitted changes
/// </summary>
/// <param name="position"></param>
/// <param name="radius"></param>
1 reference
public void SpawnObjects(Vector3 position, float radius)
{
    var stampParentObject = new GameObject("Stamp - " + name)
    stampParentObject.transform.position = position;
```

***Figure 8-49.** Filling in the summary and parameter descriptions for the method*

The generated method details are shown in Figure 8-50.

Methods

SpawnObjects(Vector3, Single)   View Source | Improve this Doc

To spawn a group of prefabs randomly around a radius centered at a position

Declaration

```
public void SpawnObjects(Vector3 position, float radius)
```

Parameters

Type	Name	Description
UnityEngine.Vector3	*position*	The center of spawn
System.Single	*radius*	The radius of the spawn

***Figure 8-50.** Generated methods details*

Basic Customization in DocFX

Now let's talk about customizing the DocFX site. With DocFX, each page is a Markdown (.md) file. Eventually DocFX will generate HTML files from them, and here are some files important to note for customization (Table 8-2).

Table 8-2. *Special Files in DocFX*

File name	Description
index.md	Index page content, the first page to show (see example in Figure 8-51)
toc.yml	Describes the table of contents. Each item can contain links to other pages or external links and can also contain subitems.

Markdown is a very lightweight markup file format for plain text, and it is very easily parsed and styled for web application. The following code and Figure 8-51 show a little example of what it looks like with a heading and list item. You can learn more about the markdown format at https://guides.github.com/features/mastering-markdown/.

```
# H1 Size Title
Hello world!
## H2 size
- Item
- Item
```

Figure 8-51. *Example markdown file*

Here is the default main `toc.yml` in the root level of `docfx_project`. You can add a custom item and reference to an external link. After regenerating, it will appear in the top navigation section (Figure 8-52).

```
- name: Articles
  href: articles/
- name: Api Documentation
  href: api/
  homepage: api/index.md
- name: Asset Store
  href: https://assetstore.unity.com/
```

Figure 8-52. *Adding a new link in the top navigation*

There are many more ways you can customize your DocFX site's style and pages. DocFX comes with a theme system, and you can apply other theme templates to your site. For more details, you can take a look at https://dotnet.github.io/docfx/templates-and-plugins/templates-dashboard.html. It's too overwhelming to cover all aspects of DocFX, but now you have a glimpse of the basic setup with DocFX for your Unity package.

Web Hosting

To host your generated static web from DocFX, there are many services you can use to deploy your site to the public. **Netlify** and **Vercel** have been my favorite go-to platforms for hosting static web applications, personal sites, or other side web projects.

To keep things simple, I suggest trying Netlify because you can drag and drop your build folder to its web console and deploy your site in a second. For a more automated workflow, both Netlify and Vercel ask you for a link to a GitHub repo and automatically build and deploy your site when there are changes to your repo, but it's a bit over the top to cover them at this stage with DocFX. Feel free to do more research on web development if you are interested.

To get started hosting on Netlify, go to www.netlify.com/ and open a new account. Next, locate your _site folder from your docfx_project (Figure 8-53).

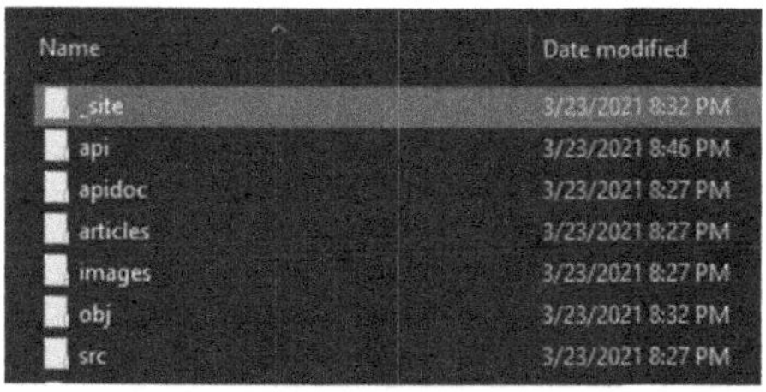

Figure 8-53. Locating your build folder (by default it is _site)

Once you reach your Netlify console (Figure 8-54), you can drag and drop the _site folder directly under the Sites tab.

Figure 8-54. *Dragging and dropping your _site folder*

Next, you can view the deploy status in the Deploys tab (Figure 8-55) by dragging in the folder.

Figure 8-55. *Viewing the deployed status in the Deploys tab*

After your site has been deployed, you can visit the URL direction (Figure 8-56).

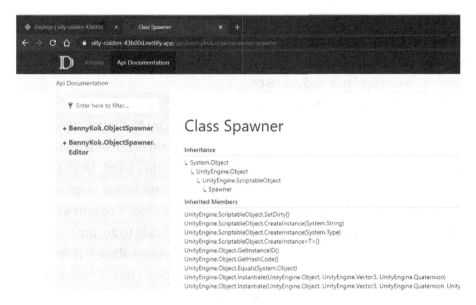

Figure 8-56. *Deployed site working perfectly!*

Conclusion

In this chapter, I talked about the basic concept of using Git to bring version control to your Unity asset projects and packages. I covered setting up a local Git repository with .gitignore for Unity and Git LFS. Next, I introduced two Git GUI clients, GitHub Desktop and Fork. You can push your local Git repository to a remote hosted by GitHub or GitLab so that you can keep track of your project in a manageable way. This also lets you collaborate with other teammates via a git remote.

Next, I talked about how using a Git submodule can increase the flexibility of your Unity project workflow, and how you can include your own asset packages in different Unity projects at the same time and easily synchronize the changes between them with Git.

After version control, I talked about the git commit message format with Conventional Commit and automatic changelog generation and package versioning with standard-version, which can help you iterate faster on asset updates and releases.

Finally, I talked about two solutions for setting up online documentation with GitBook and DocFX (hosting on Netlify). GitBook is very intuitive to use and publish your online manual/documentation for users to reference your asset/package. On the other hand, DocFX can generate C# documentation from your Unity C# projects and gives you full control over how you want to publish your site. DocFX requires more fine tuning and editing on the website before it is ready to go, but it is very useful for programmer-oriented assets or packages since it generates source documentation from your C# code so you don't have to manually include explanations of every method in your documentation site.

Further on, you can look into using GitHub Actions to automate building your DocFX site and host it directly with GitHub Pages, which could save you tons of time if you go down the route of using DocFX. GitHub Actions plays a big role in the world of CI/DI in terms of optimizing your development cycle. There is a marketplace with many community-created GitHub actions, including some Unity-related actions[3] which let you build, test, or even export .unitypackage from your Unity Project in the cloud environment.

Moving on, I will talk about publishing assets to the Unity Asset Store or sharing them freely on GitHub as an open source UPM project so others can easily install them via Git URL with UPM.

---

[3]https://github.com/marketplace?type=actions&query=unity+

CHAPTER 9

Package Distribution and Publishing

In this chapter, I will explain how to publish your UPM package on **GitHub** and distribute it with **OpenUPM** as an open-source package. Then I will cover publishing on the **Asset Store** as a free or paid asset package.

UPM Packages

As I mentioned multiple times in previous chapters, with Unity Package Manager (UPM), you can create UPM-compatible packages that can be installed and managed by UPM automatically via Git URL, Scoped Registry, and others. Therefore, besides manually exporting `.unitypackage`, now it's possible to share packages with the UPM format.

To refresh your memory, a UPM-compatible package must have a `package.json` (https://docs.unity3d.com/Manual/upm-manifestPkg. html), and you need to have asmdef setup for your runtime code and editor code. You'll usually end up with `Runtime` and `Editor` folders as suggested by Unity (https://docs.unity3d.com/Manual/cus-layout. html).

© Benny Kok 2021
B. Kok, *Beginning Unity Editor Scripting*, https://doi.org/10.1007/978-1-4842-7167-4_9

Note that publishing to the Unity Asset Store doesn't require your asset to be in the UPM format at this stage. So if you're only interested in publishing to the Asset Store, you can skip ahead to the Asset Store section, but I highly recommend you to continue with the flow since knowing how to create UPM packages gives you an advantage when the Unity Asset Store starts supporting uploading assets in the UPM format in the near future.

Creating a Local Embedded Package

In order to publish a UPM package, you must create it locally first. There are various ways to create a proper UPM package structure. The first one you can use is Unity's Package Development package. You must install the package by the package name: `com.unity.upm.develop` (Figure 9-1).

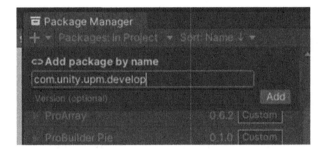

Figure 9-1. *Installing the Package Development package*

After installing it, there will be a new option in the add package dropdown in UPM, Create Package (Figure 9-2), which lets you create a UPM package directly.

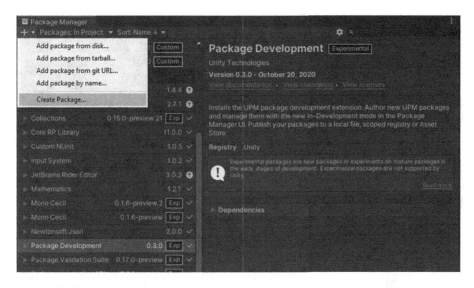

Figure 9-2. *Creating a new UPM package*

Using the Package Development package's create option will generate all the suggested directories and files for you to get started (Figure 9-3).

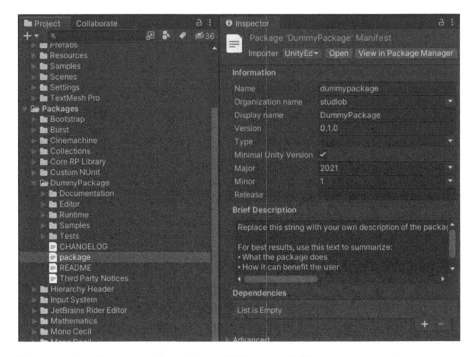

Figure 9-3. *Generated package folders and files*

And you can locate the actual package folder inside the Packages folder of your Unity Project (Figure 9-4).

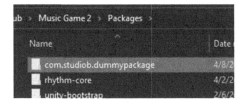

Figure 9-4. *Generated package location*

The second method is to create the package structure manually. I tend to go this route to avoid boilerplate files that I don't need at the beginning. You can start by creating your package folder in the Packages directories in your Unity project (Figure 9-5).

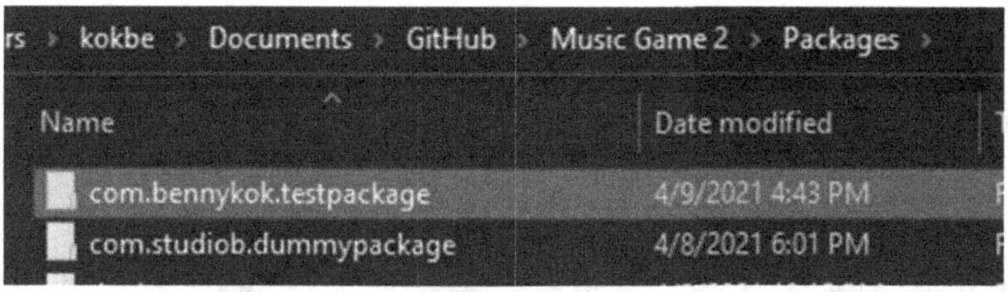

Figure 9-5. *Creating the package folder manually*

Next, to quickly create the package.json file, use the npm init command for a quick start (Figure 9-6).

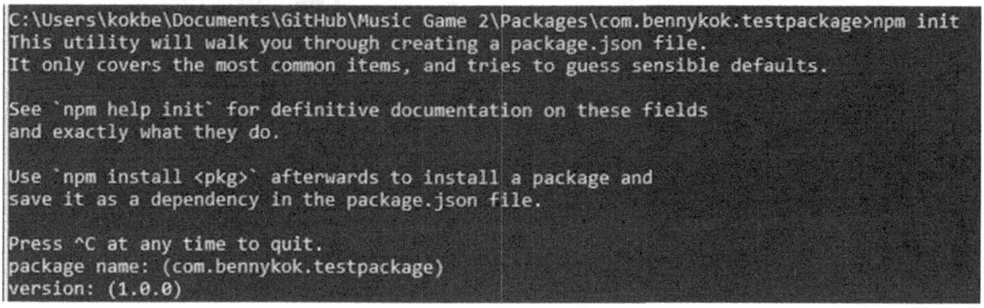

Figure 9-6. *Init a dummy package.json file*

Now, if you go back to Unity, you can edit the package.json file within the inspector (Figure 9-7).

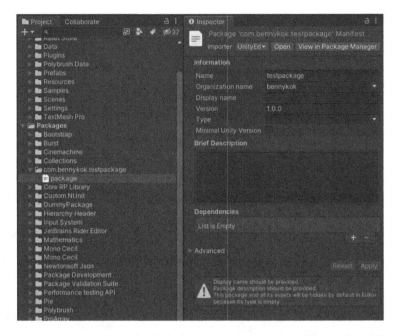

Figure 9-7. *Viewing and editing the package.json file in the editor*

Since I used the `npm init` command, there will be some extra fields in the json file which are not needed for a UPM package. Feel free to remove them (Figure 9-8).

```
{} package.json 1, U ●

Packages > com.bennykok.testpackage > {} package.json > ...
  1   {
  2       "name": "com.bennykok.testpackage",
  3       "version": "1.0.0",
  4       "type": "tool",
  5       "main": "index.js",
         ▷ Debug
  6       "scripts": {
  7           "test": "echo \"Error: no test specified\" && exit 1"
  8       },
  9       "license": "ISC",
 10       "author": "",
 11       "displayName": "Test Package"
 12   }
```

Figure 9-8. *Removing redundant package.json fields*

Now that the `package.json` is ready, go ahead and create the scripts folders (`Editor`, `Runtime`) and create the asmdef file for both directories (Figure 9-9). Then reference the runtime asmdef file to the editor asmdef (Figure 9-10).

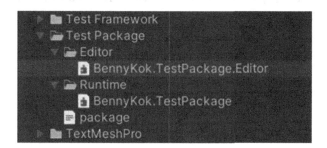

Figure 9-9. *Creating the asmdef files*

Figure 9-10. *Referencing the runtime asmdef to the Editor asmdef*

Here are some tips about managing local packages. Note that moving or copying your package folder to another Unity project's `Packages` folder will automatically add it to the project as a local embedded package. You can also zip your package as a .tgz file and install it easily in other projects via UPM's add package option.

Moving on, with your local UPM package ready, you can start integrating existing working assets into the new package or just start a blank asset from there.

Publishing to GitHub

When your local UPM package is ready, you can start publishing it to GitHub. With Git and node.js installed, you can run through the following commands to set up your local Git repo with Git LFS and .gitignore for the UPM package:

```
git init
npx add-gitignore
npx add-unitylfs
git add .
git commit -m "init commit"
```

Next, if you are ready to publish to GitHub, there are multiple ways to do so, as covered in a previous chapter on Git, but here I will talk about the GitHub CLI (https://github.com/cli/cli/), which can be installed easily with the **Chocolatey** package manager on Windows or **Homebrew** on macOS:

```
// Windows
choco install gh
```

```
// MacOS
brew install gh
```

Now you can use the gh command in your terminal of choice. The first time you use the gh command, you will need to authenticate with GitHub by the command gh auth login. This will prompt you to log in on your web browser.

Next, you can use the gh repo create command to start creating a remote GitHub repo right in your current directory (Figure 9-11). It will prompt you with options to change the repo name, description, visibility, etc. Afterward, it will automatically create the repo on GitHub and add in the remote URL to your local repo.

```
C:\Users\kokbe\Documents\GitHub\Music Game 2\Packages\com.bennykok.testpackage>gh repo create
? Repository name com.bennykok.testpackage
? Repository description
? Visibility Public
? This will add an "origin" git remote to your local repository. Continue? Yes
  Created repository BennyKok/com.bennykok.testpackage on GitHub
  Added remote https://github.com/BennyKok/com.bennykok.testpackage.git
```

Figure 9-11. *Using the gh repo create command to init a remote GitHub repo in terminal*

Finally, make sure to push to the local repo up to the remote on GitHub with `git push -u origin master`

Now that your package is live on GitHub, you can easily install the package via the Git URL in your other projects with UPM (Figure 9-12).

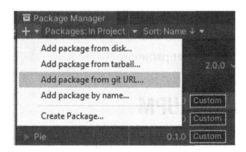

Figure 9-12. *Installing the UPM package via the Git URL*

After installing, it will appear alongside other packages in the list (Figure 9-13).

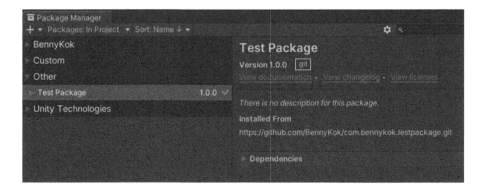

Figure 9-13. *Viewing the details of the UPM package*

If you recall from the previous chapter, you can also utilize a Git submodule and easily have your UPM package repo as a submodule in your different Unity projects. In this way, you get to version control the same package across different projects.

Publishing to OpenUPM

The downside of installing the UPM package via Git URL is that versioning on the end user side is non-intuitive. That user will need go through editing the `manifest.json` manually[1] in order to target specific Git reversions or tags. Therefore, a better solution is to have the packages available on a scoped registry. **OpenUPM** is a third-party open-source platform that provides a managed registry for UPM, CI automation from your GitHub repo, and even custom CLI for adding packages easily on the end user side.

To get a glimpse of how OpenUPM works, you can install the OpenUPM CLI from npm first as a global package on your machine:

```
npm i -g openupm-cli
```

---

[1]`https://docs.unity3d.com/Manual/upm-git.html#Git-GIT`

Next, you can browse through the `https://openupm.com/` website and look for some packages to try (Figure 9-14).

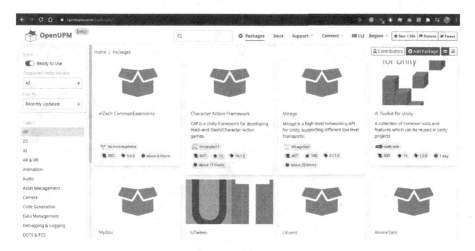

Figure 9-14. *OpenUPM website*

For example, you can install one of my packages hosted on OpenUPM by this command here:

```
openupm add com.bennykok.cmdollycart-timeline-helper
```

After that, when you hop back into Unity, UPM will start resolving the packages. The first time you add an OpenUPM package to your new project, UPM will prompt you about a newly available scoped registry (Figure 9-15).

Figure 9-15. *Prompt about new scoped registry*

If you take a look at the settings in the Package Manager, you will see the package.openupm.com has been added (Figure 9-16). So now UPM will know where to resolve the packages hosted on OpenUPM.

Figure 9-16. UPM settings

Now that you know about installing packages from OpenUPM, it is very easy to add your package to the list. Once you have a GitHub repo, as I talked about in the previous section, you can head over to the Add Package page on OpenUPM (Figure 9-17).

Figure 9-17. Adding a package to OpenUPM

Next, you can enter your GitHub repo URL. In this example, I will be using one of my open source GitHub repos. The website will fetch and prompt you to fill in missing info from the auto-detected metadata from the repo that you entered (Figure 9-18).

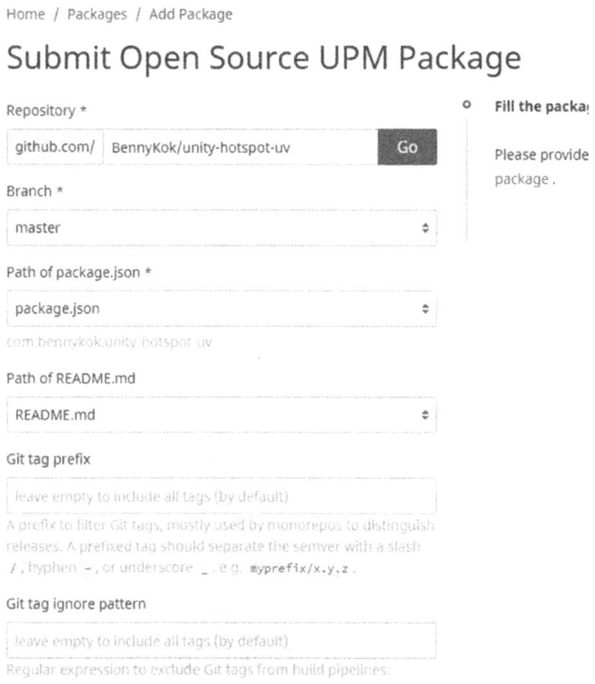

Home / Packages / Add Package

Submit Open Source UPM Package

Repository *

| github.com/ | BennyKok/unity-hotspot-uv | Go |

Branch *

| master | ⇕ |

Path of package.json *

| package.json | ⇕ |

com.bennykok.unity-hotspot-uv

Path of README.md

| README.md | ⇕ |

Git tag prefix

| leave empty to include all tags (by default) |

A prefix to filter Git tags, mostly used by monorepos to distinguish releases. A prefixed tag should separate the semver with a slash / , hyphen - , or underscore _ . e.g. myprefix/x.y.z .

Git tag ignore pattern

| leave empty to include all tags (by default) |

Regular expression to exclude Git tags from build pipelines.

○   **Fill the packa**

Please provide package .

Figure 9-18.   *Editing metadata for the package*

Next, you can review the info and proceed to submit a pull request (Figure 9-19). It will redirect you to GitHub, and you will need to continue to submit a pull request there. The way that OpenUPM works is that it will automatically merge your pull request for adding packages, and then the CI/CD will work behind the scenes to build the package and host it on the OpenUPM registry. Afterwards the website will be updated with the new entry.

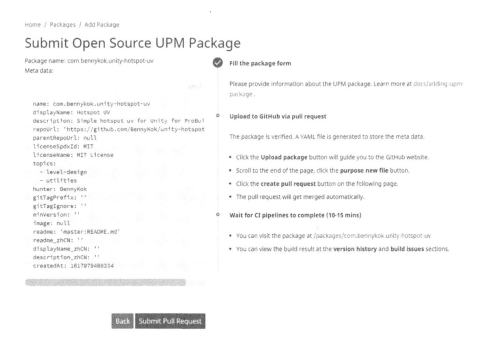

Figure 9-19. *Preview and process to create a pull request*

After OpenUPM redirects you to GitHub, you can click "Propose new file" and the pull request will be created (Figure 9-20). Note that if this is your first time creating a pull request for the OpenUPM repo, you will need to fork it to your account first, and the UI will prompt you to do so in a few clicks.

Figure 9-20. *Creating the pull request*

Usually within a day or two, your package will be live (Figure 9-21) and then you can use the openupm command to install your package.

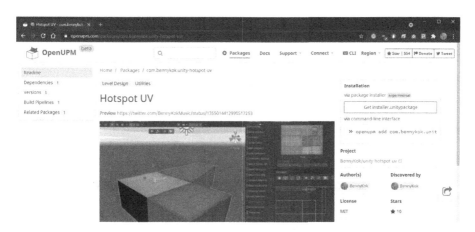

Figure 9-21. *Package details page on OpenUPM*

Unity Asset Store

Let's move on to the Asset Store, the official asset marketplace from Unity. Publishing on the Asset Store is very easy after you have signed up as a publisher, as stated in the official guide (`https://unity3d.com/asset-store/sell-assets`). I will walk you through the publishing steps via the publisher portal.

Publisher Portal

To publish assets to the Asset Store, you need to access the publisher dashboard once you have applied for a publisher account. In the current state, Unity is transitioning from the old dashboard (Figure 9-22) to the new publisher portal experience.

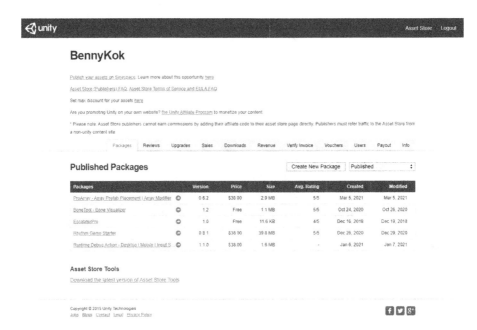

Figure 9-22. *The old publisher dashboard*

I will walk through setting up a new asset with the new portal (https://publisher.unity.com/), shown in Figure 9-23.

To give an overview, each new package must be created on the portal first. Then you fill in the information for the store page and finally you upload the actual asset package with the Asset Store Tool on your local Unity project.

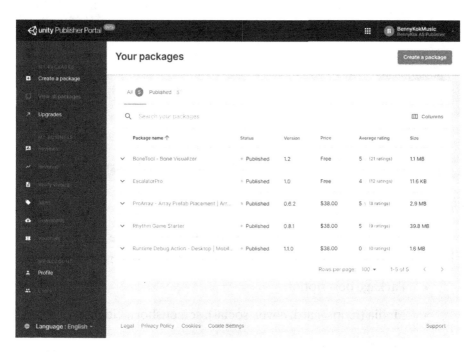

Figure 9-23. *The new publisher portal*

Drafting Packages

On your publisher portal, you can start creating a package by entering a name and giving it a category (Figure 9-24). Don't worry; both can be changed later.

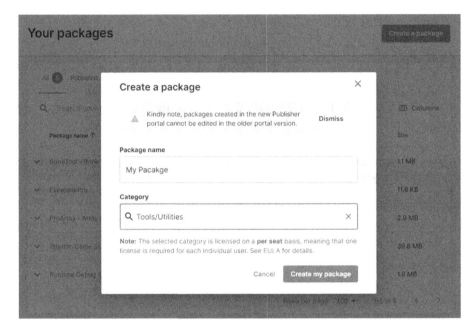

Figure 9-24. *Creating a new package draft*

Next, there are a few things you need to draft out before you can
release your package. I will go through them in the following sections.

- Package description

- Media (icons, card, cover, social), screenshots, videos

- Pricing (free/paid)

Description

With the new portal, the description part is split into three sections
(Figure 9-25) instead of the old dashboard with only a single description
section.

- Summary

- Description

- Technical details

242

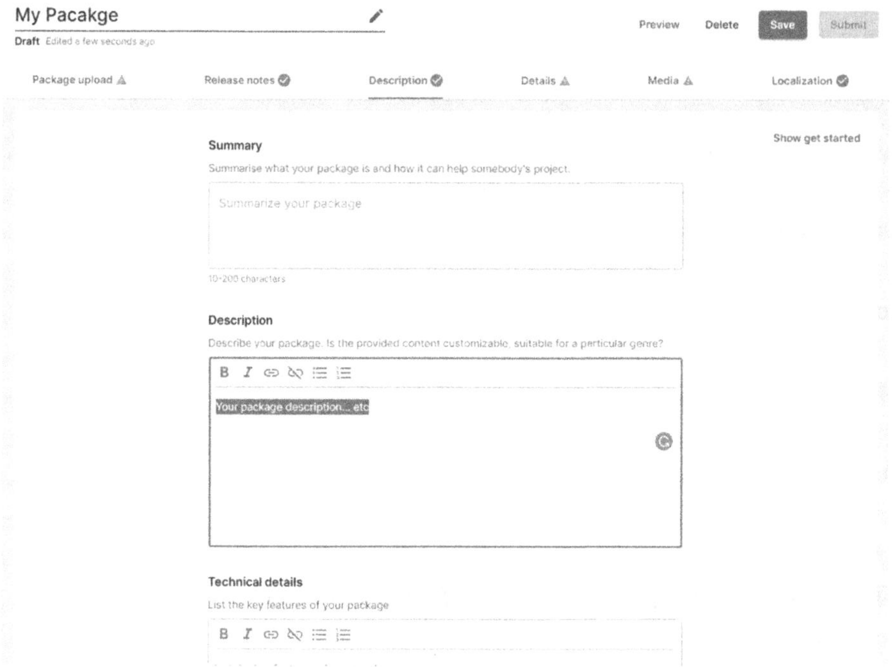

Figure 9-25. *Fill in the description for your package*

During my experiment, it is still possible just to fill in the core description part, and in the preview, the details page will only display the description, like the traditional page layout. However, by also filling in the summary or the technical details, the store page will split the description into a different section with the new layout. It also shows the SRP compatibility section (Figure 9-26).

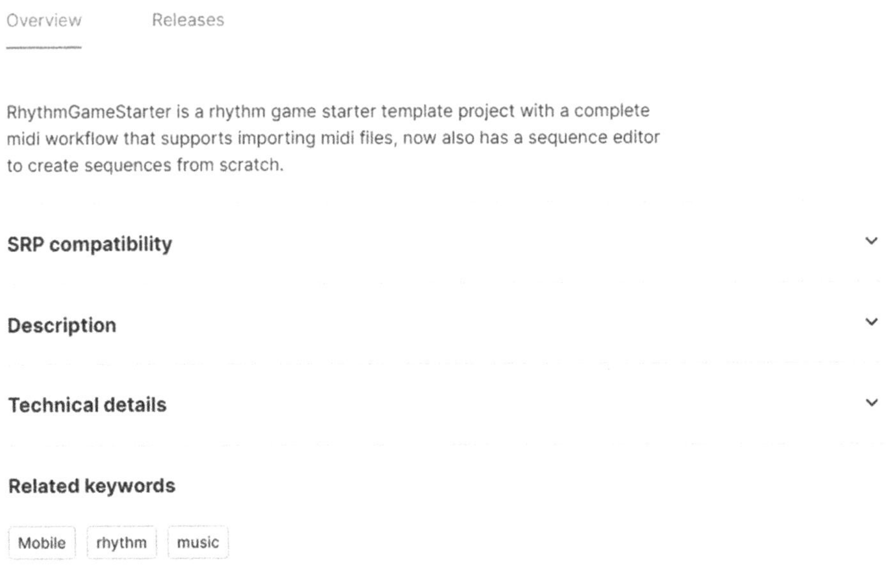

Overview   Releases

RhythmGameStarter is a rhythm game starter template project with a complete midi workflow that supports importing midi files, now also has a sequence editor to create sequences from scratch.

SRP compatibility   ⌄

Description   ⌄

Technical details   ⌄

Related keywords

Mobile   rhythm   music

Figure 9-26. *New package description page layout*

A good and on-point description will help to capture the user's attention and convey the message clearly. The best suggestion to come up with a good format for your description is to take a reference from a popular or similar asset's description. Moreover, you can now use rich text formatting to easily format the description in the draft package page to emphasize important features.

In addition, in most of my new assets' descriptions, I use an emoji next to each section title so that it gives a lively feel. Moreover, I include links to documentation, email, and my website so that users can learn more about the asset and the author. I think being more authentic and transparent gives people a better impression of your products and personal branding. This is just my two cents.

Media

For the media part, Unity provides a template[2] for each of the image specs. You must make sure the media you upload matches the required dimension; see Table 9-1.

Table 9-1. *Media Type Resolutions*

Media Type	Resolution (px)
Icon	160 x 160
Card Image	420 x 280
Cover Image	1950 x 1300
Screenshot	2400 x 1600
Social Image	1200 x 630

I used **Affinity Designer**[3] for most of my media editing for my assets. Having a nicely edited card and icon image gives a user a better first impression.

For the screenshots, I usually screen capture the special features from Unity Editor. Simply adding some subtle gradient backgrounds and large, bold text alongside the screen capture can help the features and keywords to stand out. But again, taking reference from other popular asset covers and screenshot editing is a good starting point.

After you are ready with the marketing images, just drag and drop them on to the media page (Figure 9-27).

---

[2]https://assetstore.unity.com/browse/product-page-information?utm_ campaign=as_global_information_2019-10-Asset-Store-Pub-Notice&utm_ content=2019-10-Asset-Store-Pub-Notice&utm_medium=email&utm_ source=Eloqua

[3]https://affinity.serif.com/en-gb/

Marketing images

Upload images to promote your package in the Asset Store.

Browse or drag a file here

Icon image Viewed at 100%

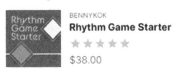

BENNYKOK
Rhythm Game Starter
★ ★ ★ ★ ★
$38.00

Card image Viewed at 100%

BENNYKOK
Rhythm Game Starter
★ ★ ★ ★ ★ (9)

Figure 9-27. *Uploading marketing images*

Lastly, you can also provide a video link from YouTube, which could be an introduction video for the package or a detailed tutorial. Having a video is more convincing since you can showcase the actual usage of your package. You get to directly communicate with the audience. Moreover, the videos you put on YouTube can also help drive traffic to the store page, and vice versa. It's a win-win situation. Beside YouTube embed, you can also include links from SoundCloud, Sketchfab, Vimeo, and others (Figure 9-28).

Screenshots & videos

Upload images (min width 1200px), videos (max size 500MB) and audio samples (max size 500MB) to showcase your package.

Browse or drag a file here

Media link

https://www.youtube.com/watch?v=bDOYN-6gdRE   Upload

Youtube, Vimeo, Soundcloud, Mixcloud and Sketchfab links are accepted

To change the order, drag the media to the desired position.

Figure 9-28.   Uploading screenshots and other media embeds

Pricing

For the pricing part, it can either be a free asset or paid asset with a minimum price of 4.99 USD (Figure 9-29).

Depending on the type and quality of your asset, it is up to you to price your work! Pricing can be stressful the first few times. You might worry that if the price is too high, it will scare off potential customers, but don't worry. The Asset Store is full of similar assets so you can take reference from their pricing and use the average pricing as a baseline for your pricing. Moreover, you can compare their features with yours, and if you feel like your asset worth more, feel free to bump it up.

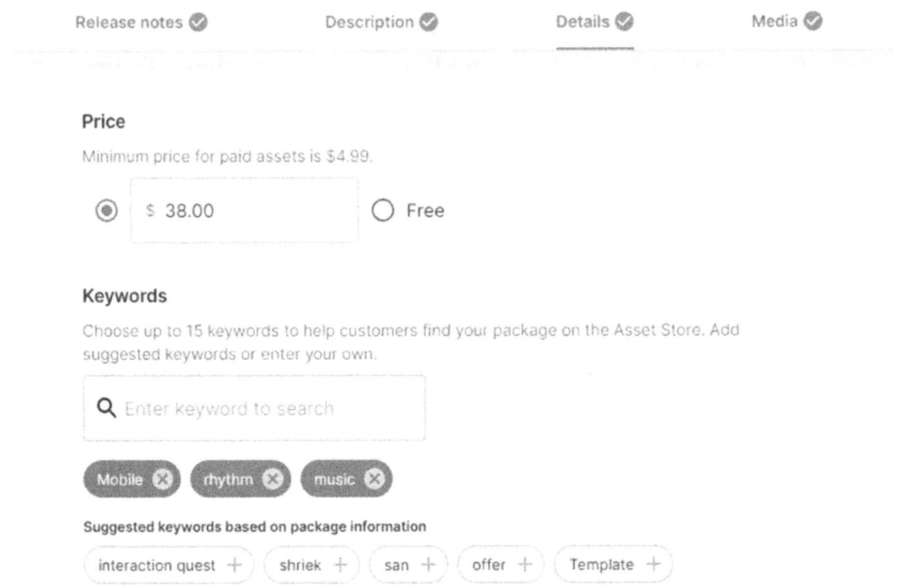

Release notes ✅   Description ✅   Details ✅   Media ✅

Price

Minimum price for paid assets is $4.99.

◉ $ 38.00   ○ Free

Keywords

Choose up to 15 keywords to help customers find your package on the Asset Store. Add suggested keywords or enter your own.

🔍 Enter keyword to search

Mobile ⊗   rhythm ⊗   music ⊗

Suggested keywords based on package information

interaction quest +   shriek +   san +   offer +   Template +

Figure 9-29. *Pricing and details section*

Uploading Packages

After you are done with your package metadata, you can start uploading the package. You must upload it from a local Unity project with the Asset Store Tool. You can also create a separate Unity project to have a final round of checking and testing before uploading.

First, you must download and import the Asset Store Tool from the Asset Store (Figure 9-30). Next, the menu item "Asset Store Tools/Package Upload" will prompt you to log in for the first time. Then you will see a list of packages that you created on the publisher portal.

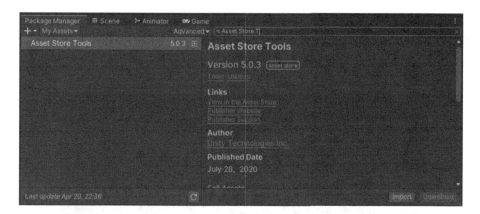

Figure 9-30. *Downloading and importing the Asset Store Tools*

Select the package you are planning to upload (Figure 9-31) and locate the correct folder for your asset. For now, your asset must be placed in the Assets folder, so if your asset is UPM-compatible and placed in the Packages folder, you will need to move it into the normal Assets folder and upload from there.

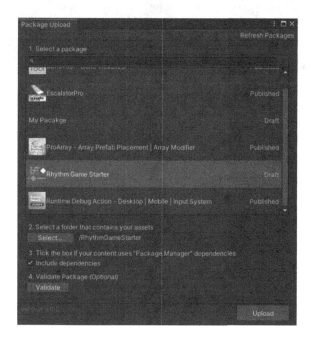

Figure 9-31. *Package upload*

Before uploading, I usually use the Validator (Figure 9-32) by clicking the Validate button to check if there are any issues with the package. This ensures a smoother submission process.

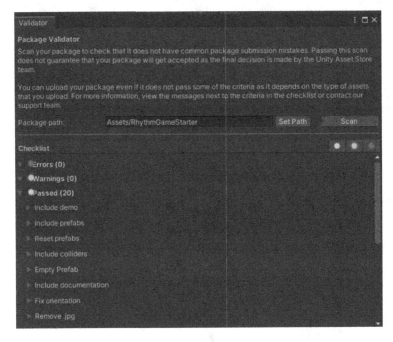

Figure 9-32. *Validator*

After uploading the package, the relative info will appear in the draft package. You must check the boxes to indicate which render pipeline your package supports (Figure 9-33).

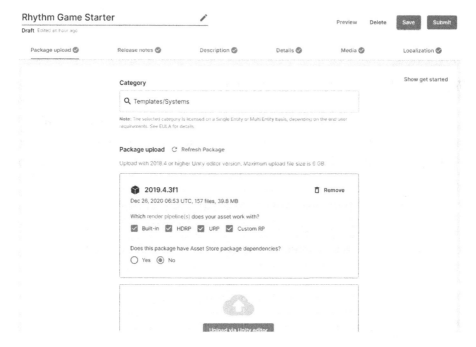

Figure 9-33. *Configuring a support render pipeline for your uploaded package*

Publisher Forum

After you have submitted your first package and it is in queue for the review process, you can apply for the publisher forum while waiting. You'll get an email about applying for the publisher forum, or you can look for the link on Unity's support site[4].

After you have applied for the publisher forum and been granted access, you can find it in the last section of https://forum.unity.com/. See Figure 9-34.

---

[4]https://support.unity.com/hc/en-us/articles/205930085-How-can-I-join-the-Unity-Publishers-Forum-

Figure 9-34. *Asset Store publisher forum*

The forum helps you stay in the loop of the latest developer news about the Asset Store development and any new announcement that is related to us, the asset publishers. There is plenty of useful information such as Unity Editor version usage stats.

Moreover, you get to ask or look for existing answers about the various publishing situations that you bump into. Hopefully someone in the community can help or someone at Unity will chime in on your specific case.

Conclusion

In this chapter you explored two ways of sharing your Unity package: UPM packages (GitHub, OpenUPM) and via the Unity Asset Store.

With the UPM package format, you can publish your open source package to GitHub, and others can install it with the Git URL via the UPM. Further on, you can submit to OpenUPM, which will provide proper versioning for your package and automatically CI/DI for your package hosted on GitHub. Others can install your package with the openupm command easily.

When publishing to the Unity Asset Store, you must prepare the store description, media (icon, cover, screenshots, videos, etc.), and proper documentation. However, you get to sell your package and earn a passive income from the Asset Store. It could be a life-changing opportunity if your package gains momentum. The more value your package provides, the more likely it will attract users. Believe me: Publishing useful assets can help a lot of peer game developers out there. It's really a win-win situation.

You saw how to distribute your UPM package and publish via the Unity Asset Store. In the final chapter, I will wrap up everything covered in this book and share some afterthoughts about being an asset publisher.

CHAPTER 10

Conclusion

You made it to the end of this book! I can't thank you enough! In this final chapter, I will wrap up the key takeaways of editor scripting in Unity and end with some thoughts and tips on how to succeed as an asset publisher.

Key Takeaways

This book covered three areas around beginning editor scripting in Unity: **purpose**, **how**, and **scale**.

The **purpose** of Unity editor scripting:

- Save development time by creating custom tools. (Chapter 1)

- Unlock new possibilities with new creative tools. (Chapter 1)

- Publish and sell on the Asset Store. (Chapter 1, Chapter 9)

How to go about editor scripting:

- Using `PropertyAttribute` (Chapter 2)

- Custom editor with IMGUI and UIToolkit (Chapters 3, 4, 5)

- Asset case studies (Chapter 6, 7)

© Benny Kok 2021
B. Kok, *Beginning Unity Editor Scripting*, https://doi.org/10.1007/978-1-4842-7167-4_10

Scale up with workflow for distribution:

- Using Git and submodules (Chapter 8)

- Automatically versioning and changelog generation (Chapter 8)

- Online documentation with GitBook or DocFX (Chapter 8)

- Publishing to GitHub and OpenUPM or the Asset Store (Chapter 9)

Afterthoughts

For me, making custom tools within Unity has been a fun and exciting journey. It's more about the "purpose" and "how" during the early development of an asset. Why would you make such a tool? How are you going to achieve this in the editor? For the "scale" part, it is more about minimizing the time wasted on development chores and how to make your package more accessible to the public with automation, so that developers can focus more on implementing new features and iterative updates for the package instead of updating the docs and versions manually.

Next, here are a few suggestions from me as an asset publisher and also a game developer.

If your goal is to create a game and eventually release it in some way, don't get trapped in the rabbit hole of overengineering the tools you have. A game doesn't need a super clean code base and super good editor tools to be a good game. In my experience, I've gotten lost multiple times because I found myself creating a whole editor tool just to solve a very specific problem, and eventually I lost track and motivation on the original game idea, and that became ProArray. It's not that you shouldn't start getting into the realm of editor scripting, but you have to keep the balance and a clear goal, whether it is actually making a game or making a tool. If you spread yourself too thin, you will probably end up nowhere.

If your goal is to publish assets, and you are just starting out or feel like you're stuck at a position where your sales are not growing as much as they could be, be patient! There are a thousand things to explore before giving up, like dabbling in new asset categories, writing shaders, or different game genre starter kits. Don't restrict yourself by just doing the things you are comfortable with. You will grow faster when you are surrounded by unfamiliarity.

From my experience, releasing Rhythm Game Starter in the beginning of 2020 was literally life changing. I had almost zero expectation of the asset, but it turned out to be my biggest success. It was my first attempt at making a rhythm game. I did tons of research beforehand and much trial and error to get to where the asset is now.

I released my first asset, ProArray, in late 2017, so it's been four years of publishing assets. It wasn't very good in the early days. You must be patient and faithful in your own path, and it takes time.

Tips

If your goal is making games or publishing assets, here are few useful tips in terms of bringing your idea to life and a strategy to grow a bigger audience.

Ideas that do not come with the right execution are never the products or games that work out. Try starting out small. Constraint the scope you are trying to achieve, or it will be too much for you to handle and the project might never get released to the public.

Fail fast, iterate more! It's important to test if people like your game or tool along the way of development. Not only will the feedback give you direction and motivation, but you will also start growing the audience around your projects. For games, share the gameplay gif online. People love seeing the indie game development process and are willing to stick around if they find it interesting! For assets, you can release a beta version on the Asset Store, so you get to see how it performs among other assets one step ahead. Iterate on it if you see potential and momentum.

Lastly, share your journey and experience somewhere! Nowadays, it's very common to see developers sharing progress of their games and tools and showing off on Twitter and Reddit. They slowly build up their online presence as they share the journey with the community. By connecting their social profile to other platforms, such as YouTube or Steam, it's very easy to drive external traffic to the platforms that they care about. So, start introducing your projects and yourself to the game dev community. You can get to know more people in this circle and grow with each other.

Further On

So what's next? Depending on your own journey and plans, it's your say! I hope you learned something from these chapters, and I truly thank you again! It's my honor to share my thoughts and experience with you.

I would like to end everything with a simple quote that inspired me the most to keep learning and striving for more:

Never settle!

– OnePlus

There may be different interpretations of this motto, but my point of view is that technology evolves constantly. If you settled where you were, you would be out of sync now. The point is to have a mindset that is open to any change and challenge. Keep the fire in your heart burning for your goals and dreams. Never settle.

Index

'nted in the United States

1ker & Taylor Publisher Services